PHYSICS AND POLITICS

PHYSICS AND POLITICS

MAX BORN
F.R.S.

FOREWORD BY
DAME KATHLEEN LONSDALE
F.R.S.

BASIC BOOKS Publishing Co., Inc.

NEW YORK

FOREWORD

When I first read these four lectures by my old friend Max Born I found them rather hard going. But he had asked my advice about publishing them and I did not want to give a snap opinion so I left them for a few days and then read them again. On the second reading I realised first of all how simply he had managed to express some very profound and fundamental ideas in physics and then how shrewd were his comments on these and on social and international affairs. I still was not convinced by all his arguments, but I found them thought-provoking and well worth the effort of studying them. It is so easy for a scientist to become narrow-minded and even to forget some of the basic assumptions upon which his own science is founded: to forget indeed that there are basic assumptions. The scientist, as well as the man of religion, lives by faith and not by certainty. Both may expect, if they have open minds, to perceive or receive new aspects of truth.

KATHLEEN LONSDALE

PREFACE

The articles collected here, apart from one, are lectures given during recent years on different occasions. They have already been published as a little book in the original German. An English version of one of them (No. 2) appeared in the English edition of the periodical *Universitas;* the same article and another one (No. 4, abbreviated) were published in the *Bulletin of Atomic Scientists* (Chicago). British friends encouraged me to make this English edition of the collection. I have chosen, as for the German book, the title of the last lecture. It is this lecture indeed which is nearest to my heart —though its central theme can also be heard in the other articles. I have made no attempt to eliminate repetitions; whenever the same subject occurs in different articles it is shown every time in another light. However, the four articles ought not to be read one after the other as if they formed a systematic presentation of the subject.

During the preparation of this book the political situation has deteriorated. I wish to emphasise that I do not think that my considerations about world politics have been disproved by these events. On the contrary, vacillations in the political attitude of leading statesmen have made these problems even more urgent.

I wish to express my thanks to the Editors of the *Bulletin of Atomic Scientists* for permitting me to use their translation, to my daughter, Mrs Margaret Pryce, for translating the second article and to the publishing firm for their careful and excellent printing. My warmest thanks are due to Professor Dame Kathleen Lonsdale and to Dr P. Rosbaud for making the publication of this translation possible. Moreover, I am most grateful to Professor Lonsdale for her suggestions with regard to the improvement of the text.

MAX BORN

CONTENTS

CHAPTER I

MODERN PHYSICS: A VETERAN'S VIEW

When I am asked about the present state and the future of physics I feel like an old captain who having served only on sailing vessels is asked to express his view on the present state and future development of steam ships. For years I have been living far from the stream of events, following the progress of science only from a distance, and hardly knowing the younger generation of scientists. However, I shall try to do my best, comparing the present situation, as far as I know it, with the times when I was still on the high seas of physical research, taking my small part in the improvement of navigation, of physical theory.

The change during these 50 years is overwhelming. Yet as far as theory is concerned I have the impression that most research still uses the same fundamental principles whose development I have witnessed. Only near to the extreme frontier of research is there any indication of new ideas. Everywhere else relativity and quantum theory still reign supreme.

Each of these theories is characterised by a certain absolute constant, relativity by the velocity of light, quantum theory by Planck's constant, the quantum of action. Now it is very likely that to understand elementary particles (electrons, protons, neutrons, neutrinos, mesons, and hyperons of divers kinds) a new absolute quantity will have to be introduced. Years ago, in an attempt to improve the classical theory of the electron I suggested an alteration of the laws of the electromagnetic field which would abandon the principle of the undisturbed superposition of fields (this would be called a non-linear theory); and for this purpose an absolute field strength was introduced. But this attempt was premature, as it was made before the experimental exploration of processes between particles of high energy. These investigations brought to light an enormous number of new facts, and there are now modern unitary theories which try both to represent these facts and to take proper account of relativity and quantum theory. Among these theories that of Heisenberg seems to be the most ambitious and important; it is non-linear and introduces an absolute length. But I am not competent to describe the physics of the future, still less to express an opinion about its merits.

Meanwhile many important discoveries have been made which can be explained in terms of current and generally accepted theories, but which also indicate the trend of future developments. I shall mention only two of them. One is the demonstration that space has less symmetry than was formerly believed. It used to be taken as evident that space is homogeneous and isotropic; i.e. that each point in space is equivalent to any other point, and each direction in space to any other direction. Moreover, we were convinced that the so-called law of parity holds, which means that two configurations of mirror symmetry, like right and left hand occur equally often in nature. This has been refuted by striking experiments on processes between elementary particles. Any future theory of these particles must take account of this fact.

Another set of discoveries is concerned with the so-called anti-particles. According to the theory of relativity it is to be expected that to each particle there belongs another one which is identical with it apart from one fundamental property which has the opposite sign. This property may be its electric charge. It was known for many years that the negative electron has a positive counterpart (positron), and it was expected that the heavy proton which in our matter always carries a positive charge, similarly has a negative counterpart.

2

This too has been discovered recently. But the neutron, an uncharged particle, also has an anti-particle, to define which would however be beyond the scope of this article; this anti-neutron has also been found.

These results suggest speculations about the possibility that distant systems of stars (galaxies) might exist which are totally composed of anti-particles. It can be shown that in these systems among the reversed properties of matter would be that of deviations from parity: if "right" is more frequent than "left" in our galaxy, there it might be the other way round. Thus in the end parity might hold if the whole universe were considered. If a particle collides with its anti-particle they annihilate one another with a release of energy much larger than anything we know from nuclear processes. It is possible that certain catastrophes in the Universe, the appearance of new stars (novæ), can be explained by assuming a collision between matter and anti-matter. It is not likely that these extremely powerful processes could be made useful for human purposes. At present we have enough to do with the technical exploitation of the well-known nuclear fission and with the exploration of the much stronger process of nuclear fusion which at present is only used in the hydrogen bomb for military purposes. In these fields of research the current theories of physics are essentially sufficient. They are there-fore growing rapidly in many directions, and physicists of all nations participate in this work in peaceful competition. They know exactly how the laws of relativity and quantum theory have to be applied in each case.

It might be thought, therefore, that these fundamental doctrines, half a century after their discovery, would be perfectly consolidated and generally accepted. Though this is true in general the discussion about the principles has not completely died down. In my youth the opposition came mainly from philosophers who raised well-founded objections to relativity and could be seriously answered; to-day the opponents are mainly representatives of political ideologies whose resistance to the new concepts of space and time due to the theory of relativity and of reality and causality due to quantum theory derives from dogmatic prejudices. Those who accept the communistic ideology of dialectical materialism regard the interpretation of these theories accepted by the physicists as "idealistic" and therefore they reject it. In the West there is an inclination towards an exaggerated positivism which goes to the extreme of denying reality to the external world. As scientific research does not take much notice of these disputes they would be of no consequence were not dialectical materialism a kind of National Religion in the Eastern countries. The Soviet physicists have done brilliant work in this difficult situation and refuted infringements from the ideologists. On the other hand, Western positivism has not caused much damage, since it is obviously rather difficult for a physicist, as for any other person, to live in a world whose existence he claims not to believe in.

Refuting extremes and rigid systems does not mean objection to any philosophical interpretation of physics. On the contrary, physics is only alive if it is conscious of the philosophical significance of its methods and results. Physics has received much from traditional philosophy, but has also returned some gifts. Before Einstein no philosopher had any idea that the concept of simultaneity of events might be problematic, or that there could exist something like curvature of space. Nor have philosophers ever ventured on such criticism of the principle of causality as is involved in the quantum theory.

A few of the subjects studied in different branches of physics which have advanced in a spectacular way during the last years may be mentioned here: atomic nuclei; the solid state; electric discharges in a highly ionised gas, so called plasma (used for the production of very high temperatures); crystal magnetism (used for the production of very low temperatures). All these disciplines are highly extended, intimately connected and interwoven. It would take up too much space to indicate what the actual problems are. The rate of progress can be seen from the following. The highest temperatures marked to-day are about 10 million degrees while some years ago, when I was still in academic life, they were about 5000 degrees. The lowest temperatures reached to-day are of the order of one-millionth of a degree absolute, compared with about 1 degree absolute ($-272°$ C.) in my day.

Physics has expanded in such a way that nobody is able to survey the whole. The following data give some idea of it: *The Encyclopedia of Physics* (being published by Springer) is planned to have 54 volumes, each of them between 300 and 1000 pages. Nobody knows more than a small fraction of this enormous amount of material. Yet it goes on increasing from day to day, and many a volume may be already outdated on publication. Still more terrifying is the accomplished fact, that the *Transactions of the International Congress on the Peaceful Uses of Nuclear Energy*, held in Geneva, 1958, are now published in 27 volumes, many of 500, some of 800 pages. Each volume addresses specialists of a narrow section of this special branch: nuclear physics. This boundless increase of material is common to all sciences. It is caused not only by the continuous expansion of research inside the older group of civilised nations, but through participation of newly developing nations all over the world.

Thus the very meaning of the concept "knowledge" has undergone a fundamental change. It does not refer any more to a single person but to the community of all men. While the total of what has been found and deposited in print grows in an unlimited manner that part of it which an individual can possibly know and handle becomes relatively smaller and smaller. Thus the gigantic increase of knowledge of the human race as a whole may mean that individuals become more stupid and superficial. There are unfortunately many indications that this is actually happening.

5

This is one of the great social problems of our time for which, as far as I see, no solution has yet been found. Organisation may be of some help in the amassing of purely technical information; true and deep knowledge depends, by its very nature, on the single enquiring mind.

Connected with this is a fundamental change in the organisation and working of physics, namely in the relation of science to the state and, more generally, to human society: the size and the cost of the instruments used demand thorough organisation and team work; thus science can be financed only through public funds and becomes dependent on governments.

Even when I began to study, about 1900, the time of self-made apparatus constructed from sheet metal, wires, glass tubes and sealing wax was almost gone. Reliable instruments could be obtained from industrial firms, and with their help the physicist built his apparatus, still, however, using wire, glass tubes and sealing wax. The cost of an experimental set up was rarely more than £100. There existed some more expensive instruments, like big concave gratings in optics, but they were used only by a few specialists.

Since then the magnitude, complication and price of the instruments have steadily increased, and with good reason. It is a consequence of the magnitude of the atomic energies with which we have to deal. My youth fell into the period when the external electronic structures of atoms, on which the ordinary physical and chemical properties of substances depend, were being explored. The energies involved, measured in the conventional unit electron-volt (eV) are represented by figures of the order 1 to 10. In the subsequent period of nuclear physics we have to do with millions of eV (meV) and to-day, in the exploration of elementary particles with billions (thousands of millions). Now the main method of research consists of bombarding one kind of particles with another and to observe the effect of the collisions. Thus the "guns" used, the accelerating machines, have incessantly increased in power

6

until they have reached fantastic dimensions. As an example I give some data about the, at the time of writing, largest instrument in the world. It stands in the neighbourhood of Geneva, Switzerland, and is owned and run by the European Organisation for Nuclear Research (Conseil européen pour la recherche nucléaire, CERN) to which 13 West-European countries belong, among them Great Britain. The accelerator is a rather narrow tube, forming an enormous circle of 200 metres diameter, highly evacuated and surrounded by 100 electro-magnets which deflect the particle beam and keep it along the central line of the tube. The particles are protons which reach 29×1000 meV by acceleration in single pushes. One proton push carries per revolution up to a million million protons, and these revolve 480,000 times per second which corresponds to a path of about a quarter of the distance from the earth to the moon. The final velocity reached at 25×1000 meV is 99.99 per cent. of the velocity of light and the mass of a proton is increased, according to the well-known relativistic effect, by a factor of 25. The building costs of this instrument were about £10 million. The yearly budget of the whole CERN establishment (which contains several other big instruments and installations) was in 1959 £4½ million. A similar instrument producing a somewhat bigger acceleration (30×1000 meV) is under construction in Brookhaven, U.S.A., and expected to be ready soon. The biggest machine at present actually running in the U.S.A. is in Berkeley, California; it has a radius of 80 metres and produces 6.3×1000 meV. The communist family of nations has a big research centre at Dubna, near Moscow, where an accelerator with a radius of 58 metres produces 10×1000 meV. A still bigger instrument planned for 50×1000 meV is under construction.

Even the biggest telescopes, once the most expensive instruments of science, are relatively cheap. However it is possible that astronomy will catch up again through the construction of radio telescopes, which are steadily growing in size.

Institutions like CERN, Dubna or Brookhaven are, of course, employing a great many people, not only physicists proper, but auxiliary workers from neighbour sciences, in particular engineers. The machines can only be used to capacity if they work without interruption, and each special apparatus attached is so complicated that a group of experts is needed to run it. Thus research work is no longer done by individuals but by teams. Already in my time there existed something like team work. Students working for a doctor's degree in a laboratory were collected in groups on related problems, each group led by a senior scientist, the head of the department or one of his assistants. But usually this group leader was so predominant in knowledge and experience that the purpose of the combined effort actually consisted in working out his individual ideas.

How this is to-day with the big machines I cannot say as I have never taken part in this kind of work. Yet I must say that I find it difficult to understand how a scientific personality can freely develop in what is essentially a school of narrow specialists. If one looks at the results, the amount of good, even excellent work done in the frame of the fixed programmes is amazingly large; however whether this method will ever result in a breakthrough to totally new ideas can be doubted.

Even smaller universities and technical schools have to-day instruments of a size and price unheard of in the old days. Here too the students working on doctor's and other degrees are organised in teams.

Theoretical physics has not escaped this tendency. The mathematical methods are so complicated that specialisation cannot be avoided. For larger projects, which involve several branches of physics this leads again to team work. An example is found in the electronic computers—electronic brains—which need a staff with special technical training. The theoretical individualist is a rarity to-day. Einstein did his greatest work alone and in spare hours from his occupation as a clerk of the

Swiss patent office in Berne. Could a new Einstein be expected under modern conditions?

While the big acceleration machines are built solely for research, reactors are used for both research and production of electric current, isotopes and fissionable material. They are very expensive, too, and can be run only by team work.

Why are all governments willing to grant large funds for these gigantic projects? Some, like Great Britain, are moved by a concern about exhaustion of coal reserves, others by the desire to become independent of the import of coal and oil. But in the world at large there are fossil fuels sufficient for centuries to come. What statesman ever really cared to plan so far ahead?

Actually it is the military applications of nuclear energy, the A- and H-bombs which entice the cash from the Treasury coffers. The statesmen have recognised physical research as a source of power and are therefore prepared to subsidise it. In the United States, army, navy and air force are extravagant patrons of physical science, and they assist not only research of immediate practical application but also investigations into fundamental problems whose application to practical questions is not immediately evident. They have learned from the history of the atom bomb. Will this dependence on the armed forces in the long run be good for science?

There is a branch of physical research which is still more expensive than nuclear physics: the exploration of space. Its main instrument is the rocket. With its help gravity has been overcome, a terrestrial object transformed into an astronomical one and thus Newton's celestial mechanics experimentally demonstrated. A rocket has reached the moon; soon human beings will travel there, and perhaps to other planets as well. There are rocket enthusiasts who even regard a journey into cosmic space, beyond the planetary system, as possible. Quite a number of things about space in the neighbourhood of the earth have been found, things of some scientific interest—hardly as yet of any practical value. The technical knowledge and skill applied to all this is magnificent and deserves the admiration which is accorded to it. But the expense is just as stupendous. According to Saenger the United States Government spends about 4 billion dollars annually for the development of rockets, the Soviet Union about twice as much. For comparison let us look at a few figures for aid given to underdeveloped countries during the years 1955-1958: from U.S.A. altogether 4·4 billion dollars, of which about a quarter was for military purposes, the rest for economic assistance. From the Eastern Block altogether 2·8 billion dollars, of which about a third was for military purposes, the rest for economic assistance. Thus we spent on economic help each year a total of about 1·3 billion dollars, a small fraction of the 12 billion dollars spent on rockets.

Why are sums of this order available for this kind of research? Mainly because rockets are of military importance. If they can reach the moon they can also carry atom bombs from one continent to another. They are a weapon in the fight for power between the big nations, perhaps the most important one. Space journeys have also a considerable propaganda value. Some years ago I took part in a conference of space travel experts where not only physical, technical and medical problems were discussed, but also theological and juridical ones. Some of these things were interesting, others absurd, so absurd that I was induced to give a short address in which I expressed my doubts and scruples. Since these have not diminished during the years I would like to quote some sentences from this speech; they refer to what seems to me the essential motive for space travel.

"Space travel is an exercise of the human desire for adventure, of the impulse to try to transcend acknowledged boundaries, like climbing Mount Everest, expeditions to the North or South Pole, etc. In short, it is a sport, which to-day is of military importance and therefore promoted by the political powers in being. I can see no other sense in it. But it is an extremely expensive sport, an extravagant luxury, except for big business which profits from it. I cannot see that space travel contributes anything to the material welfare of human beings, to say nothing of their true happiness and security. I do not believe that words like these will stop the current of events. Still I think that they ought to be spoken lest later generations, if there are any, look back on our age as wholly mad. I myself was taught to distinguish intellect from reason. From this standpoint space travel is a triumph of intellect but a tragical failure of reason."

All this I still maintain to-day. But it does not exhaust the problem. I realise this from the address given by the British statesman, Philip Noel Baker, on the occasion of his receiving the Nobel Peace Prize.

After stating that in the nuclear age disarmament is a necessary condition for the survival of the human race, he said that the main obstacle to it is this: atom bombs once fabricated can be easily concealed and shielded against control because there is no method of detecting their slight radioactivity from sufficiently large distances. Therefore Noel Baker proposes to outlaw the main means of delivering the bombs, namely rockets, because their production and storage can easily be controlled.

This step however would obviously hit space travel. Imagine what a row would be raised by the space enthusiasts who are perpetually popularising their projects and exploits in books and periodicals, especially in those read by the young: prohibition of rocket research would be called lopping off the most luxurious branch of science, a blow to progress, and so on.

They, and all of us, ought to be clear that objections of this kind will obstruct and may well prevent any agreement of the atomic powers about nuclear disarmament.

Here the ways of people diverge. There are those who are in favour of continuing traditional power politics, and others who regard this as absurd in the atom age and try to replace it by something better. Defence against atomic weapons is impossible, war means national suicide and is therefore plain insanity. The present peace is based on mutual deterrence, and is therefore completely unstable. There is much talk about disarmament, but not the least progress has been made. On the contrary, the armament race continues unabated.

The physicists are well aware that their work has brought the world to this crisis. Many of them feel their responsibility heavily. They do not wish to be simply tools in the hands of politicians but to take part in great decisions, at least as consultants. In several countries therefore societies have been formed whose aim is to inform their members about atomic science in relation to political problems, to advise governments and to try to promote rational decisions. In the United States there is the Federation of American Scientists (FAS), in Great Britain the Atomic Scientists Association (ASA),* in the German Federal Republic the Vereinigung Deutscher Wissenschaftler (VDW), and similar societies in other countries which all have the same purpose. In America there is moreover a Society for Social Responsibility in Science (SSRS), whose members agree not to take part in any armament or war work.

The aim of all these societies is not the advancement of science but the overcoming of dangers which the human race has to face as a consequence of science. The bombs of Hiroshima and Nagasaki have been called another "Fall of Man", of scientific man, or the loss of innocence of free research. Everybody knows that it is not enough to strain the intellect in order to penetrate deeper and deeper into the secrets of nature if this means producing ever more powerful weapons of mass destruction. We have to use our reason and ask: to what purpose? And as only an expert knows what is happening,

* The ASA became the Atomic Scientists Committee of the British Association for the Advancement of Science in 1959 and its functions became more educational and less political.

12

what can be done, which effects must be expected, the answer cannot be left to the statesmen, nor to philosophers, theologians, historians who think in rigid, traditional ways. We must be listened to.

Does this retrospective review give any indication of what will happen in physics during the next 50 years?

Leaving fantastic descriptions of future discoveries and inventions to the writers of science fiction, I foresee two extreme possibilities.

If the human race survives the next 10 or 20 years without a great war there will come into being a world organisation transcending national states, which will guarantee peace. Then physics will be highly honoured because, by producing terrible means of destruction, it will have made clear the absurdity of power politics and war.

If however the great war breaks out there will be nothing left of physics, nor of civilised life in general. After a period of unimaginable misery and suffering there will follow either the silence of the grave, or a new hard beginning. This may lead upwards; but there will be a curse upon science and no physics for a long time to come. Perhaps it may rise again. Then it is to be hoped that the new human race will make better use of it than we do to-day.

It is our task to help to avoid the second alternative. This is no physical problem but it is at present more important than new triumphs over the forces of nature.

CHAPTER 2

THE CONCEPT OF REALITY
IN PHYSICS

I. *Introduction*

Sixty years ago, when I went to school, we were taught that physics is that part of natural science which concerns itself with the properties of inanimate matter and the laws which apply to it. The "real" world of physics thus consisted of the things around us, with the exception of living organisms. Even at that time, this definition seemed rather superficial. In each physics textbook used in school, we met in the first chapter, dealing with mechanics, concepts which did not represent things, such as forces, energies, and so on; and in the subsequent chapters, in which light, electricity, and magnetism were treated, as well as in those dealing with heat, concepts of this kind predominated more and more: ether, electro-magnetic fields, temperature, to name but a few.

Already at that time many thinkers, physicists as well as philosophers, wondered whether these concepts correspond to something "physically real", or whether they are only a kind of auxiliary, logical instrument. As years went by, the insufficiency of the primitive definition of physical reality became more and more obvious; not only because the tangible concepts of matter, bodies, and things were gradually replaced by more subtle concepts such as fields, electrons, and so on, but also because of a peculiar duality which has arisen in physical science. The physicist uses in his laboratory, to-day, as of old, apparatus and instruments which consist of metal, glass, and other ordinary substances. These are for him "real things", in the same sense of the word as are things everybody uses in daily life. What he observes are changes in the position or state of such things. However, he speaks of his observations in an entirely different language, in which the real components of this apparatus play only a very subordinate role, or no role at all. He speaks of atoms, nuclei, electrons, mesons, fields, and their properties and states—properties moreover which do not resemble at all those of ordinary bodies. From the point of view of our daily experience with material things, these properties appear strange, even impossible. It would not be correct to say that physicists fall into two groups—on the one hand, the experimentalists, who use the ordinary concepts of things, and on the other hand, the theorists, who speak in that abstract language. Often it is the other way around. When I, a theoretical physicist, am conducted through a modern physics laboratory, I encounter the following difficulty: a young experimentalist shows me his results—combinations of instrument readings arranged in tables or diagrams, or blackenings of photographic plates. However, he speaks about these results in words which pertain to some atomic or subatomic processes, to electron transitions or nuclear transformations, without noticing that for me, the visitor, the relation between what he shows me and what has been revealed by these experiments is by no means obvious.

Apparently physics has now two sets of realities. To learn physics means not only to assimilate the techniques of both of them—of experimenting and theorising—but also to master the two corresponding languages. We have to know when to use each of them, and we must be able to translate from one into the other. Certain rules exist for doing so; these rules can be learned and used without further analysis of their meaning. In practice, this is enough to carry out physical research. It is, however, clear that such a dualism does not satisfy a philosophical mind. From times immemorial, the human spirit has yearned for a complete unified picture of the outside world.

Physics appears to the layman mysterious and uncanny, not only because it produces technical miracles, such as television, atom bombs, artificial satellites, etc., but also because it is such a dual world, containing on the one hand solid instruments and machines, and on the other hand invisible entities with incredible properties. When he hears that the physicists describe a cathode ray sometimes as a stream of particles called electrons and sometimes as a sequence of waves, he is inclined to ask—with some justification—What, then, are these rays in truth?

To answer this the physicist must leave his usual level and repair to a higher observation point. He must investigate the philosophical foundations of his methods of reasoning and attempt to give to his apparently divergent and in fact non-visualisable concepts, a foundation which could satisfy sound common sense.

II. Multiplicity of the Concept of Reality

Before discussing solutions of the problem suggested above, I would like to say something about one point which could lead to a misunderstanding; namely, the lack of single meanings in our language. The word "real" is used in our everyday language with many different meanings. When somebody tells me a story, and I ask him, "Really?" I mean "Is what you are telling me true?" When a politician says he is pursuing a "realistic" policy (Realpolitik), he means that in his actions he takes into account all the existing political motivations and forces without prejudice. The "realities" of a peasant are his fields and his village; those of a workman his factory and his street; those of a musician, his orchestra and the sounds it produces. In this case, the word "real" is used in the sense of "important" or "standing in the centre of existence". I shall do my best and try to define the concept of reality so as to make it free of all these connotations. Furthermore, certain philosophical systems and religions teach that only the spiritual world is real; and the physical world is a semblance, a shadow without substance. This point of view is of great philosophical interest. It is, however, outside the scope of our considerations, which are to deal only with physical reality. Of course, this physical reality, too, reaches us only through the intermediary of an act of thinking. However, what interests us here is not this mental act, but its object, the things which we consider real— even when we attribute to them properties not possessed by things of our daily life (including physical instruments). The aim of the following considerations is to illuminate this difficulty.

III. Positivism and Materialism

I will deal mainly with two schools of philosophy which play an important role in our time, positivism and materialism. In a certain sense, these are two opposite extremes of interpretation, each emphasising a different point of view. I would like to say from the outset that I do not agree with either of these two philosophical systems. Rather, my views include some aspects of both of them, with some additional points.

It would be proper to begin here with a short definition of positivism and materialism. This is, however, extremely difficult, because in the course of time these systems have undergone considerable transformation. In the case of positivism it is not, however, impossible to describe its fundamental teaching. It consists in asserting that the only real things are the experiences through which man has lived. All concepts and constructions used in daily life (or in science) to interpret these experiences are artificial products, having no counterpart in reality. They have been invented in order to be able to establish reasonable, logical connections between different experiences, and to predict future ones. The adherents of this teaching differ, however, rather widely in the interpretation of what is "experience". Some of them, for example the well-known Viennese philosopher and physicist Ernst Mach, who influenced Einstein, mean by this bare sensations. From this point of view, even the concept of the table before me has no reality, but is an artificial auxiliary concept, bringing into mutual relation innumerable and always different, but somehow connected sensations. Others think that this goes too far, and that one must consider as directly given reality the totality of our sensations organised into "things". Others loosen this definition still futher. For example, the physicist Pascual Jordan, who emphatically calls himself a positivist, says that the immediate reality consists of the facts of observation, whether in daily life or in experimental science. This last version seems to me to have very little in common with positivism proper. I would call this point of view empiricism, since it means not much more than to say that physical theories must be in accordance with observations, a statement which appears to me rather trivial.

True positivism must deny either the reality of objective existence of the external world, or at least the possibility of making any statements about it. One would think that no physicist could hold such opinions. Yet they do, and they are even fashionable. Pronouncements of a positivist character are found in the writings of almost every leading theorist. For example, H. Dingle, now Professor Emeritus of history and philosophy of science in the University of London, said in a lecture about the contemporary position of physical thought (published in *Nature*, vol. 168 [1951], p. 630): ". . . we must regard physics as the progressive establishment of rational relations between the results of our measurements. From this point of view the quantities with which physics concerns itself are not evaluations of objective properties of parts of the external material world; they are simply the results we obtain when we perform certain operations." He illustrated this statement by examples; he pointed out that physicists used molecules as "counters" or "dummies", and thus denied them any reality.

I opposed this point of view in an article entitled "Physical

Reality", which appeared in the *Philosophical Quarterly* (1952, p. 129), and which was later reprinted in my book, *Physics in My Generation* (London: Pergamon Press, 1956, p. 151). This book made my anti-positivist attitude known in the Soviet Union. A Russian scientist, Professor Sergei Suvorov in Moscow, translated my article into Russian and published it together with a critical article of his own. He kindly sent me the papers and supplemented them by explanatory letters. It was a great pleasure to me to be able to enter into a direct and friendly exchange of ideas with a communist scientist, in an area in which philosophy and physics meet, and where the situation is relatively simple and clear, at least compared to that encountered in economics, sociology, and politics.

Professor Suvorov designates the group of Western physicists who have participated in the conceptual construction of modern atomic theory as the "Copenhagen school", because it was Niels Bohr, the great Danish physicist, who has explored with particular persistence and success the philosophical foundations of physical theory. Suvorov counts me as one of this group, although as a matter of fact, I have been to Copenhagen only a few times on short visits. The fact that I agree with Bohr's fundamental ideas, above all with his "complementarity principle", is the result of my own thinking, although I am quite aware that mine was only an afterthought, stimulated by Bohr's forethought.

The "Copenhagen interpretation" of physics is unacceptable to Suvorov because he regards it as positivist. He supports this assertion by quotations from the writings of Bohr, Heisenberg, Jordan, and others. All of them did make statements, which, as I mentioned before, belong to the positivist sphere of ideas. However only a few, in particular Jordan, have expressly proclaimed their allegiance to positivist philosophy as a whole.

In Marxist terminology, positivism is a subjectivist and idealistic teaching; such teachings are rejected by materialists.

Professor Suvorov approves therefore of my rejection of positivism, and interprets my arguments from his point of view. He then states with regret that I reject also materialism. He attributes this to the fact that I am familiar only with the obsolete, "vulgar" materialism of the last century, and not with the dynamic "scientific" materialism of our time, which, according to him, gives a satisfactory interpretation of modern physics in the broad frame of the communist conception of our world. I am grateful to him for a description of the fundamental ideas of this modernised materialism.

I would like to explain my attitude in this question. I must, however, remark that such considerations, whether they deal with positivism or materialism, are not physics. They do not belong to the realm of strict empirical science, but are, as is often grandiloquently said, "Problems of philosophical attitude". Personally, I am inclined to consider them problems of common sense. Since I believe I have a little of this quality, I am going to talk about these questions without pretending to develop deep philosophical thoughts. I have tried to supplement by reading the outlines which Professor Suvorov gave of the new materialism. I am naturally not in a position to support my conclusions by quotations from authorities beyond all criticism, as communist authors do by quoting Marx, Engels and Lenin. What I present is my personal opinion, not that of a school.

IV. Positivism

The question whether the positivist attitude towards life in general is justifiable cannot be quite avoided here, although we are concerned with physics. Physics consists not only of concepts and theories: it deals first of all with experiments with ordinary materials, carried out by ordinary men who understand each other in their work by means of ordinary words. As an activity, physics is part of ordinary life, and a collective activity.

Extreme positivism, which recognises only the impression of senses as real, and considers everything else to be artificial constructions invented to establish logical connections between these impressions, is obviously the opposite of a philosophy suitable for collective activity. It is, on the contrary, highly subjectivistic. It can even be called solipsistic. It is well known that this attitude cannot be either proved wrong or defended by logical arguments, except perhaps in conversation with oneself—since a possible discussion partner would be himself only a construction, not a reality. However, immunity from the proof of logical fallacy is only a purely negative criterion of correctness.

In fact, every experimental physicist treats his instrumentation as if he were a naive realist. He takes its reality as given *a priori*, and doesn't rack his brains about it. Niels Bohr has made this attitude the basis of his whole philosophy of physics. In fact, he goes one step further. He considers the application of classical mechanics to instruments to be as self-evident as the use of everyday speech. Otherwise, any mutual understanding of physicists about their individual activities would be impossible.

We have seen, however, that physics operates not only with instruments, but also with concepts, such as forces, fields, atoms, electrons, and so on. Some of these have the character of objects or things, others not; but they all have one thing in common: they do not belong to the everyday world, and they are derived indirectly from the analysis of experimental results. Often they have been first introduced through theoretical considerations; in some cases, they have later become increasingly accessible to direct observation, and so increasingly "real"—think, for example, of chemical molecules, which to-day can be photographed by means of electron microscopes.

This question arises: Is this perhaps the place where a positivist attitude imposes itself? Should we not deny the reality of "things" postulated in microphysics, and consider them only

21

constructions useful to establish logical connections between observed events?

The reasons which positivists use to defend this point of view are of two kinds. In the first place, they say, we deal here with such small dimensions that direct realisation of the existence of these "things" and their immediate observation are out of the question. Therefore, they say, things on the atomic scale are only mentally constructed mathematical models. In the second place, in order to permit a complete description of the phenomena, interpreted by means of these models, the latter must be invested with properties which no object of ordinary experience has ever been found to possess.

Before putting forward objections to such statements, I would like to point out that consistent positivism is bound to declare the world of stars an equally "unreal" model world. The stars are, for the ordinary observer, only small points of light, whose radiation can be extended into a spectrum. All assertions concerning their size and their physical properties are based on mental contemplation, and on calculations. It is not much different with the sun and the moon and the planets. We know that the presently accepted model of the planetary system is only a few centuries old; that before that entirely different models were current. Yet, do not such arguments sound silly to-day, in the age of sputniks and explorers? A dog has already departed on a cosmic trip, and men have followed suit. Certainly all our theories begin as models: but a well-chosen model has a content of truth which becomes more and more apparent as research advances.

Let us return to the micro-world. Here, too, the theory evolved from observations has provided first a rough model, then increasingly finer ones, with a growing content of truth. In fact, there is no sharp limit between the everyday world of large-scale phenomena and the micro-world. A crystal of common salt certainly belongs to the ordinary kitchen world. We can grind it to a fine powder, with particles too small to be seen with the naked eye. To see them we need a lens; and when they become still smaller, a microscope. Are the particles of the powder therefore becoming less real? To see still smaller particles, such as those that occur in colloids, one can use an ultramicroscope; and when this instrument fails, one takes an electron microscope, which—as I have already stated—penetrates down to molecular dimensions. What we really see in it are the electrons scattered by the particles under observation. The instruments which permit the "observation" of the interior of molecules, atoms, and ultimately, of nuclei, and the determination of their structure are, in principle, based on the same phenomenon of scattering. Where is then the limit between the tangible world of our senses with their "reality", and the micro-world which a positivist thinks is only a construction?

This brings us to the second argument of the positivist. He would say that such a boundary exists. To interpret the observations, we are forced to attribute to the things in the micro-world properties which are radically different from those of ordinary bodies, and altogether incapable of direct visualisation.

The laws of the cosmos, as well as those of the atomic world, fall into two great framework theories, the theory of relativity and the quantum theory. According to the theory of relativity, the length of an object is not something definite as it appears in the ordinary everyday world, but depends on the relative velocity of the object and the observer. The same is true of mass. Time, too, is relative. Two observers having identical clocks, but moving relative to each other, make different estimates of the duration of one and the same process. Professor Dingle concludes from this theory that length, mass, and velocity are not properties of a "real things", they are useful conceptions that permit the establishment of logical connections between different observations.

We will now look at the atomic world; there the situation

is quite similar. However, before I deal with this somewhat more complicated question, I would like first to state my own point of view, which is as follows: Physical models have a definite content of truth, which is not essentially different from that of the things in daily life. Here I must make some general remarks.

V. Widening of Concepts

My first remark concerns the transformation of concepts, in particular their widening.

That many concepts of daily life change their meaning in time is a banality. They adjust themselves, as it were, to changed conditions. Think of the word star which to-day is more frequently used to describe a film actor than a celestial body. However, let us leave the vast field of daily language and turn our attention to science, first to mathematics.

The concept of a number at first referred to counting: 1, 2, 3, 4, and so on—the whole number, the integer. Later, the concept was extended to include fractions, such as 2/3, 4/5, and so on. Then roots, such as $\sqrt{2}$, transcendental numbers such as π, and imaginary numbers such as $\sqrt{-1}$. Already the ancient Greeks knew the proof that $\sqrt{2}$ cannot be represented as a fraction, that is as a quotient of two integers. It is a new concept; and the same thing is even more true of π and of $\sqrt{-1}$. Yet, all these things fall to-day under the term, "number". The justification lies in the fact that these "generalised" numbers share with integers most, though not all, of their properties. In other words, with a few precautions, it is possible to use them for calculations according to the same rules.

The same principle is used in geometry. In analytical plane geometry we introduce an infinitely distant point on every straight line and can then say that parallel lines intersect "in infinity". The behaviour of different bundles of parallel lines can be described in a simple way by assuming these artificial points lying on an infinitely distant straight line. Thus in formulating the laws of intersecting straight lines exceptions are avoided. We then invent non-Euclidean geometries which operate with points, straight lines, and planes, but differ in certain respects from ordinary geometry. Finally, we arrive at generalisations of the kind of Riemannian geometry in which the concept of a straight line has no place at all, and is replaced by that of the shortest (or "geodetic") line. We see here that the continued use of old terms has a limit, imposed by the structure of the things investigated.

Exactly the same is true in physics. We speak of ultra-sound, which we cannot hear, of ultraviolet and infra-red light, which we cannot see. We are so accustomed to extra-polations into regions where our sense organs fail that we have stopped thinking of the original meaning of the concepts of sound and light.

We use the same freedom when we face the phenomena of the atomic world. We call an electron an elementary "particle" because it has many, even if not all, of the properties particles exhibit in the tangible world.

VI. Invariants

My second general remark has to do with the concept of real things, which we must now consider more closely.

For a normal human being, the world is not a kaleidoscopic sequence of impressions of his sense organs, but a constantly changing sequence of interconnected events, in which certain things retain their identity despite their ever-changing aspects. This capacity of the mind to disregard the variation of the sense impressions and to sublimate out of them something constant and invariant appears to me the most impressive of our spiritual endowments. We see a bird close by in all details; it jumps from branch to branch, and soon soars into the sky as a small dark spot. And yet, we always see the same bird. Modern psychology describes this fundamental aspect of human perception under the heading of "Gestalt" psychology. I know something about it, because I once had close relations with some of the founders of this theory: Köhler, Hornbostel, Wertheimer.

This psychological teaching—that perception has the property of "wholeness", so that the whole appears to be more than a simple sum of individual impressions—has a counterpart in the physiology of perception. In this field of research, too, I am not an expert; but I have made an effort to get acquainted with its results; for example, by reading the Waynflete lectures of the English physiologist, E. D. Adrian. Each nerve fibre whether it belongs to the sensory or to the motor system, whether it carries sensations of taste, sight, hearing, or heat from the periphery of the body to the brain, or inversely, motor impulses from the brain to the muscles, does it in basically the same way. It transmits regular sequences of electric pulses which have nothing—absolutely nothing— in common with the source of the excitation. When these periodic pulses arrive in the brain, they are conducted to different specific areas, according to the course the fibre takes in the brain tissue. There their monotonous but complicated message is decoded and converted within an incredibly short time into a picture. The brain thus carries out, with amazing speed, a process which can be described as solving the problem of the invariant properties of the coded nerve message. The result is not a chaos of single, unorganised impressions, but the perception of whole things and structures.

From all this, we can conclude that single sense impressions are not what the positivists believe to be the "primary data", but abstractions. What are actually given are certain invariant characteristics of the sense impressions, which we describe as "objects", or "real things". A mental process is needed to dissolve them into single sense impressions. We must keep this fact in mind in an attempt to develop a philosophy of science. It makes no sense to go back to disjointed "sense impressions" as the raw material of physics. In this way, we would not be able to understand one another even in respect of the simplest instruments and manipulations. What we must start with are everyday things, and words of everyday language.

A real problem first appears when we go out of the range of natural sense impressions and use enlarging devices, such as microscopes or telescopes, or electro-magnetic amplifiers, combined with photographic registration methods. We then encounter a new situation in which everyday experience doesn't help us, and where our brain ceases to be capable of extracting invariant traits, bearing the character of "things", from the mass of individual observations. Whoever has been shown something in a microscope by a medical friend will know what I mean. He sees only a chaos of coloured specks and contours where the trained eye of the medical research man recognises microbes or other familiar objects. This is precisely what every investigator experiences when he penetrates into a new field. He perceives something that at first seems to have no meaning; he searches for invariant traits, persisting through many special observations, and so arrives at an interpretation. This achievement is not subconscious and effortless, like that of the child in the face of impressions of daily life; rather it requires full employment of the powerful apparatus of the science already secured—in physics, above all, through mathematical analysis.

Mathematics has concerned itself extensively with the problem of invariants for the last hundred years, and mathematical physics has taken over its methods and conclusions. When in geometry we apply the Cartesian method of a "co-ordinate system", we determine geometrical structures through their projections on the axes (or planes) of coordinates: if we change the system of coordinates, we obtain other projections. These measurements and numbers are therefore only very indirect descriptions of the investigated bodies; they give their relationship to the chosen reference system. The properties of these bodies, which are independent of the system of co-ordinates, i.e. the invariants, must be derived by thinking. The great mathematician Felix Klein has organised and classified all mathematics from this point of view.

VII. Physical Invariance

Exactly the same is true in physics. Analytical mechanics and the field theories are formulated in the language of co-ordinates. The conclusions one derives are, however, supposed to belong to a hypothetical reality, even if they are not descriptions of this reality, but of its relationship to the chosen reference system. The properties of the postulated physical reality, which are independent of the reference system, are the invariants which can be obtained by the analysis of coordinates or projections.

One complication arises however in physics, and that is that the magnitudes which appear as invariants in one period of knowledge, and are therefore considered there as representations of "reality", lose their standing in other periods. An example is the transition from classical mechanics to relativity. According to Newton, distances, time intervals, and masses are invariant in respect of transformation from one mechanically "legitimate" reference system (inertial system), to any other such system. These concepts fail, how-ever, in the field of electrodynamic and optical processes. I cannot enter here into considerations which led to Einstein's theory of relativity. I can only say the following: Einstein, too, postulates the existence of inertial systems—that is "permis-sible" reference systems, in which the fundamental equations of physics appear in their simplest form. However, the relationship between these systems as expressed by the so-called "transformation equations" are, according to Einstein, different from those assumed by Newton. Time and space coordinates are coupled in them into an indissoluble unity.

Distances, time intervals, and masses as defined before are no longer invariants, but projections. In their stead there are now other invariants, called "rest length", "proper time", and "rest mass". If these are used, one again obtains symbols which are suitable for describing material realities.*

Things are, in principle, similar in quantum theory, although the situation there is more complex and difficult to explain to those without special knowledge. I will try to give at least a hint. We have to deal here again with a failure of classical mechanics, on a level which is perhaps even deeper than that on which the theory of relativity had to be introduced. In dealing with atomic systems, it is no longer possible to make statements such as: Under such and such conditions, this and this will happen. It is only possible to say: Under definite conditions there will be a definite probability that this and this will happen, another probability that that and that will happen, and so on. The predictions of the theory are not deterministic, but statistical, and they apply not to a supposedly objectively occurring process as such, but only to situations produced by conscious experimentation. However, despite this entry of a subjective element into the study, each experiment provides a contribution to objective statements. It can be said—and it corresponds exactly to the mathematical structure of the theory—that every single experiment is a projection of reality. Think, for example, of the elliptic shadow which a circular object such as a dinner plate throws on the wall. By observing this shadow, we obtain no convincing proof of the circular shape of the original object, or of its dimensions; this conclusion can be, however, derived from observation of several such shadows on different walls. Each single shadow thus contains a contribution to the knowledge of reality, and a sufficiently large number of shadow-casting experiments

* In the transformation theory of physics there appear not only invariants which correspond to properties of things but other quantities called co-variants which are used to describe fields. These have also a kind of reality but in a more abstract sense which will not be discussed here.

conveys the complete reality. The latter is something invariant, independent of the projections. Exactly the same thing is valid for atomic experiments and their quantum-mechanical interpretation. A single experiment provides, in general, no conclusive knowledge of reality. However, from a well-organised series of experiments, we can derive invariants, attributable to real things, exactly as the brain derives them, unconsciously, from nerve signals.

In pre-quantum days it could be imagined that we might (in principle and even in practice) improve a single experiment so as to make it reveal the complete reality. We could, for example, throw simultaneously several shadows of the same plate on different walls and derive from this single experiment the shape and diameter of the plate.

The new thing in quantum mechanics is the denial of this possibility. Quantum mechanics says, for example, that the location and the velocity of an electron cannot be determined simultaneously and exactly. The more precisely we try to measure one of these quantities, the more uncertain the other becomes. This is Heisenberg's famous uncertainty principle. The different situations created by experimentation are, as Niels Bohr says, "complementary". The complete reality of the situation can never be grasped; but, after all, who wants to know it? Through systematic creation of conditions for the performance of different experiments, we can, however, again arrive at invariants, at common qualities and quantities. For example, by making complementary experiments with negative or positive rays, we can obtain sets of invariant magnitude associated with these phenomena: charges, masses, spins, numbers. This is enough to permit us to talk of electrons or ions as particles of a definite kind, using the previously explained principle of the widening of concepts. These particles are no longer like particles of grain or dust. True, under certain conditions of experiment we can directly see the paths of individual particles; many have seen the atomic tracks observed in the cloud chamber, or traces produced in fine-grained photographic emulsions. On the other hand, these particles have no individuality. For statistical purposes, they must be counted in a different way from the way in which ordinary objects are counted. In large numbers, they lose their particle character altogether and produce interference phenomena, which make one think of waves. Mathematical theory can describe all these phenomena without inconsistency. Ordinary considerations fail, however, if we try to use it to obtain a unique picture with properties in every aspect similar to those with which we are familiar from large-scale objects. If, however, we give up this hope, the quantum theory provides us by the intermediary of its invariants with a picture of reality satisfying all reasonable needs.

VIII. *Materialism*

I now come to materialism, as presented by Professor Suvorov. As I have already mentioned before, he agrees with my objections to positivism, but he thinks that the idea of invariance does not answer the fundamental epistemological question, "What is reality?" He distinguishes between appearance and substance (the latter being probably what Kant called "Ding an sich"), and he states that, "The modern materialism, in generalising the development of science in all fields, says that to know an object means to discover the objective relationships which are specific for that object". He then proceeds to give two examples of physical objects which have been discovered on the basis of this criterion, the anti-proton and the anti-neutrino. He asserts that the measuring of certain invariant properties, such as mass and charge, do not suffice for their identification, but that the latter requires other "specific relationships". The anti-proton, for example, is a negatively charged particle of the same mass as the ordinary positively charged proton; it can be confused with the negative hydrogen ion (a proton with two electrons).

To distinguish between the two, we have to note that the anti-proton keeps its negative charge, while the hydrogen ion loses relatively easily one or even two electrons. We have therefore to make a theoretical estimate of the probability of such electron loss, and decide whether such a change of charge is to be expected under certain conditions. However, this ionization probability is obviously another invariant, not of the anti-proton, but of the hydrogen ion. If anybody wants to use the term "specific relationships" to designate the totality of invariant properties associated with a particle, I do not object—except that this is a somewhat vague, nebulous term, which together with the slogan "materialism" belongs to the last century.

In the lifetime of Marx and Engels, nothing was known of to-day's relativistic and atomistic physics. The concept of the atom was used only in chemistry; but there atoms were merely symbols used for calculation ("counters" or "dummies" according to Dingle), not real things. Matter was at that time what our senses conveyed it to be; physical measurements dealt with the sensually perceivable properties of things. To-day the situation is quite different. Matter as given by our senses appears a secondary phenomenon, created by the interaction of our sense organs with processes whose nature can be discovered only indirectly, through theoretical interpretations of experimentally observed relationships; in other words, through a mental effort. To designate the result of this operation by the old word "matter" seems to me wrong.

I have just called the expression "specific relationships" nebulous. I would like to dwell briefly on this subject. "Specific" must mean "characteristic for a certain object". In the past, some relationships could be so described. Chemists believed in the permanence of elements, in their incapacity to change. Hydrogen and oxygen thus did have specific properties. To-day this is an obsolete idea. All elements consist of the same ultimate components, nucleons and electrons, and can be converted into each other. There are no specific laws valid for a single atom any more; atoms of every kind are, in principle, describable through a solution of the general quantum mechanical many-body problem. Of course the elementary particles themselves, the nucleons and electrons, as well as protons, neutrinos, mesons, and hyperons, are now being characterised by specific relationships. This is, however, obviously only a temporary state of science. Einstein, Eddington and others have attempted to develop a unified, all-inclusive theory. They failed, because they did not possess all the necessary empirical foundations for their theory. To-day it is different. We now have a good general knowledge of elementary particles, of their properties and transformations; and the all-inclusive theory also may be already there; I mean the spin theory of elementary particles recently announced by Heisenberg and Pauli. This theory has raised as much excitement among physicists in the Soviet Union as it did in the West. Physicists of the whole world understand each other well, despite differences of official ideologies. However, the fact that the new unified theory was proposed in the West and not in the East may be not entirely unrelated to the restriction of free thinking in the East, caused by the existence of an official philosophy. Distinctions based on the scheme "materialism versus idealism" do not correspond with the facts of our time.

It is my hope to be able to reach an understanding on this question with Professor Suvorov. Our differences are slight, and due in part merely to his use of the traditional language of Marxism, which to me is alien and appears insufficient. Incidentally, at the end of his consideration he quotes that ominous assertion of Marxist philosophy that "Objective laws exist in society which are specific for a given society and independent of human conscience". This principle of "historical materialism" is the real root of the conflict between East and West, because it is the basis of the fanatical belief of

Marxists that the world is bound to fall to them spontaneously and inevitably.

This belief is a descendant of the physical determinism derived from Newtonian mechanics. There it looks as if the laws of nature should permit us to predict, with absolute certainty, all that is going to happen in the future, if only the initial state is fully known. In recent years I have made some efforts to demonstrate the fallacy of this deterministic interpretation of classical mechanics and of the whole physics derived from it. I believe that my arguments have been absolutely strict and convincing. No physicist, either in the West or in the East, has as yet discovered an error in my arguments. Determinism presumes that the initial state is given with absolute precision. Given the smallest margin of uncertainty, there will be a point in the development of events from which prediction will become impossible. The concept of absolute precision of physical measurements is obviously absurd, a mental abstraction created by mathematicians to simplify the logic of their systems of thought. It belongs as little to physics as do all other statements which are in principle not verifiable—for example, absolute simultaneity in the theory of relativity, or the rotation period of an electron in Bohr's atomic theory. The principle of elimination of empirically meaningless statements has nothing to do with positivism, although an association between the two is being asserted both by adherents and by the enemies of this philosophy. It is a heuristic idea, which has proved its worth in all parts of modern physics.

To come back to determinism: In a detailed investigation, together with my co-worker, Dr. Hooton, I have established what kind of predictions are possible, and which ones are impossible, in a very general mechanical system, provided no assumption of absolute precision is made. The result is that determinism is out of the question in the original sense of the word, even in the simplest classical science, that of mechanics.

34

This conclusion does not depend on the special assumptions of quantum mechanics. In this way, the whole idea of determinism vanishes. To apply this idea to historical events is simply fantastic. At the time of Marx and Engels, under the influence of astronomical predictions, it was possible to believe in mechanical determinism—although there was no reason why this problem should not have been looked into more deeply even then. To-day no scientist should make obeisance to determinism—of which historical materialism is an offshoot.

IX. *Conclusion*

Language difficulties—and age—do not permit me to go deeper into the study of the Russian literature on these problems. I am therefore especially grateful to Professor Suvorov for his attempt to act as a mediator. Lately I came across another work which I could read, and have to a large extent read. It is a French volume, *Physique*, in the collection Recherches Internationales à la Lumière du Marxism (No. 4. September-October 1957). It contains nine papers, all arguing against the so-called Copenhagen School of theoretical physics. Most of these papers have appeared in other places (partly also in other languages), and many already have been answered in detail. It seems unnecessary to do so again here. There is only one point I would like to mention. The fourth article in the book (p. 71) contains a polemic by M. Bunge against Professor L. Rosenfeld, once professor at Manchester, and at present director of the Northern Institute for Nuclear Studies. Rosenfeld is an enthusiastic follower of Niels Bohr, but he also proclaims his adherence to dialectical materialism. In several papers, he has tried to represent Bohr's complementarity concept as giving support to Marxist philosophy. Since this concept reconciles the controversy between corpuscular and wave theory, Rosenfeld sees in it a striking example of the dialectic development as defined by Hegel: a struggle between thesis and antithesis, leading to synthesis. Mr. Bunge rejects

35

this idea with the greatest vehemence and declares Bohr's philosophy of complementarity to be incompatible with dialectic materialism. I quote this only to show that the Marxist dogma is not quite established even among its supporters. How should we outsiders find our way?

I venture to presume that the opinions of leading Soviet physicists are quite similar to ours. As an example, I can cite a paper by an outstanding Leningrad theorist, V. A. Fock, who in the twenties worked with me in Göttingen. This article, written in English, bears the title " On the Interpretation of Quantum Mechanics" and represents the so-called Copenhagen view clearly and unambiguously, rejecting in particular the attempts to salvage determinism which have been undertaken by de Broglie and his school (as well as some others, for example, in the above-mentioned French book). Fock merely makes the concession to official philosophy by describing the new ideas as a dialectic development of materialism.

The main aim of my consideration is—and I hope I have made this clear—to show that philosophical dogma should have no place in the interpretation of natural science, and that conversely physics is not a proper basis for the derivation of such dogmas. The claim of Marxism to be a scientific interpretation of the world (in fact, the only valid scientific interpretation) represents a danger to mankind. There is a similar danger in the arrogance of the liberal capitalistic West, which calls itself Christian, but in its politics pays no attention to Christ's teachings. I do not believe that Jesus would have approved of defending Christianity with atom bombs. The letters of Khrushchev and Dulles, stimulated by Bertrand Russell's appeal and published in the *New Statesman* early in 1958 are ominously reminiscent of theological controversies of the 16th and 17th centuries. Each party defended his dogma, praised the excellence of his system, and denounced the horrors of the other. At that time, the controversy ended with the catastrophe of the Thirty Years' War, and the devastation of Germany. To-day, in the age of the atom bomb, the whole world would be devastated, if the field were to be left entirely to dogmatic politicians.

I hope that physicists can make a contribution toward international understanding by renouncing the extreme ideas of positivism as well as of materialism. Above all, we must make away with the fairy tale of physical determinism and thus also with the spectre of historical inevitability.

CHAPTER 3

THE LIMITS TO OUR IMAGE OF THE UNIVERSE

I. Introduction

When I was thinking about the subject of this lecture I remembered, from my school days, some of Schiller's verse:

Thoughts can as close companions live together,
But things will hit each other hard in space.

These lines might serve me as a text to-day.

Thought believes itself limitless; nothing impedes it as long as it remains pure thought. However, when we consider things in the real world, this does not hold good any longer. Things do jostle each other in space.

Physics, with its sister sciences of astronomy, chemistry, crystallography, geology, etc., tries to construct a mental image of the world of things, and meets barriers everywhere. The conceivable and the actual do not always coincide.

It is about these barriers which physics itself discovered, that I shall talk first.

Physics is, after all, only one science among many, and science only one activity of the human spirit among many. What are the thought barriers of physics as seen from this wider standpoint? These are questions which cannot be answered by the methods of physics. I shall not avoid them, but shall give my opinion about them.

II. The Principle of Impotence. Theory of Heat

Every law of nature, in a certain sense, creates a barrier; that which contradicts it is unattainable. This statement has proved itself, in a way, reversible: When experience meets a barrier which it cannot penetrate in spite of great effort, then this is the key to new positive knowledge, a new law of nature, as we call it.

A British mathematician, Sir Edmund Whittaker (formerly a colleague of mine at the University of Edinburgh) believes this heuristic principle to be so important that he has given it a name: the "principle of impotence". This principle applies when there are, in an existing theory, statements about concepts (such as simultaneity of events at different places) which cannot be verified empirically. There is no place for such concepts in the system of physics; they are eliminated or altered as the new law demands it.

The oldest and most forceful example of this heuristic principle is the perpetuum mobile. Countless inventors have tried to construct a machine which will produce work from nothing—always in vain. In the end this failure was recognised as a law of nature. Thus the principle of the conservation of energy was formulated; this has remained a fundamental concept of physics to this day, and has proved itself extremely fertile. It is the first, and the most important, of the so-called "conservation laws" which occur in all the branches of physics and seem satisfying to us because they correspond to the old proverbs which say "Owt for nowt", or "You don't get something for nothing". The conservation of energy was first proved experimentally for the conversion of work into heat, by Robert Mayer and Joule. We owe its general formulation to Helmholtz.

The second law of thermodynamics was similarly established by Carnot, Clausius, and William Thomson (later Lord Kelvin). They based it on general negative experiences such as the fact that heat never moves from a cooler to a warmer body, or that it is not possible to convert all the heat in a body into work without other changes taking place. Were this possible, we would be able to pump heat out of the ocean and would thus have a virtually unlimited source of energy, a perpetuum mobile of the second kind, as it is called.

This is another "inability" leading to a law of nature, which has proved to be just as fertile as the law of the conservation of energy. The second law does not maintain the conservation of a quantity, but only says that a certain quantity, called entropy, never diminishes. In this way we can treat mathematically phenomena in which heat is converted in an irreversible manner.

As a result there arose a new, wholly unexpected scientific barrier. For the second law implies the existence of an absolute temperature, independent of the thermometric substance, which can be determined from every empirical scale by thermal measurements; and this temperature has an absolute zero. It lies at $-273°$ in the centigrade scale. It is impossible to go below this point, and all attempts at further cooling are in vain. Many experiments have proved this. But this barrier, too, has caused an enlargement, not a limitation, of our experience. For in the region of absolute zero we discover that the behaviour of matter is altogether different from the normal. I shall mention only two such phenomena: Firstly the loss of heat capacity by all bodies at very low temperatures, secondly the so-called superconductivity. Many metals become perfect conductors around temperatures of $1°$ absolute. A current produced in a closed circuit can be shown to exist hours after the electromotive force has been cut off. Now we have approached very much closer than $1°$, to within nearly one millionth of a degree of absolute zero, but I cannot enlarge on the queer things which happen then.

However exciting the discovery of a limit to cooling, it was soon made comprehensible by the kinetic theory of heat. This states that heat is produced by the concealed and ransom movements of the molecules. So there obviously must exist a state without heat content, in which all the molecules are at rest. The further development of the idea of heat as the random movement of molecules demanded the introduction into physics of statistical methods and concepts, particularly of the probability of a state. Entropy, according to Boltzmann, is a certain measure of this probability, and its tendency to grow is plausible enough, if we remember that order easily becomes disorder, but not the other way round. Absolute zero was thought of as the state of perfect rest and order. Modern research has shown that this is not quite correct. Quantum theory (*cf.* section VI) requires the existence of motion even at zero temperature and this "zero-point energy" has been confirmed by experiment.

III. Special Theory of Relativity

It is very instructive to search physics for further examples of this heuristic principle of impotence. But it is not very important which—in order of time—came first, the failure of all attempts to achieve something new, or the formulation of a new law of nature which explains this failure.

The theory of relativity can be interpreted in the one way or the other. Electromagnetic and optical processes are transmitted through a vacuum. It was naturally assumed that space devoid of ordinary matter is filled with a finer substance called the ether, which carries these phenomena. Light is then explained as waves in the ether. The earth moves through the ether, and just as we feel a draught in a moving car, so there ought also to be an optically discernible ether-draught on earth. Light waves would take longer to cover a certain distance against the ether wind than in the opposite direction. However, highly refined experiments (especially those of Michelson and Morley) have shown that this is not so.

Great scientists, such as Lorentz and Poincaré, partly succeeded in explaining this by altering the existing laws of the electromagnetic field. But the situation only became clear when Einstein took as his starting point the inability to observe the ether wind, and raised to the status of a principle the fact that the speed of light does not depend on the movement of the observer. This contradicts, of course, our accepted concepts about movements. But Einstein saw that these are physically untenable as they contain a vicious circle. For in order to determine the speed of light we need synchronised clocks at different places; the clocks, however, can only be synchronised by light signals if we know the speed of light.

From this critique of the concept of simultaneity by Einstein and Minkowski there followed a revision of our ideas about time and space, as well as of the laws of mechanics and of the electromagnetic field. Consequences of this have been proved by experiment over and over again. I shall only mention one in order to show how restriction of knowledge in one direction may lead to extension of knowledge in another. It concerns the so-called dilatation of time which has been much discussed lately in connection with space exploration. A space traveller leaves the earth, travels at great speed to a distant fixed star, and then returns to earth. This may have taken ten years of his life; but when he arrives on earth he finds that, in terrestrial time, hundreds of years have passed. There were many who called this assumption by Einstein absurd, but at the time not much notice was taken of it. To-day, however, when it seems that space travel will soon be within the grasp of technology, voices are again being raised against the idea. From the point of view of physics it is, however, arguable from experimental facts that twin brothers, one of whom makes a space journey while the other stays at home, will not be the "same age" when they meet again, and that their bodies and minds will have aged at a different rate. (Whether it will ever be possible for men to make a journey long enough to test the point directly seems to me doubtful.)

I want to refute most strongly objections which have been raised in the name of ontological criticism.* It is said that

* Two books known to me expressing such objections are: Friedrich Dessauer, *Naturwissenschaftliches Erkennen*, Beiträge zur Naturphilosophie (Frankfurt 1959), and Nicolai Hartmann, *Philosophie der Natur—Abri der speziellen Kategorienlehre* (Berlin, 1950).

physical observations, and the statements derived from them, do not refer to a real space and real time, but only to the manner in which we obtain such physical knowledge, namely by measurements with the aid of light. It is supposed to be of decisive importance to distinguish between the "metric", and the "existential", the ontological. As far as I have been able to understand the teaching of the ontological philosophers, "ontological" means that which we experience by direct apprehension, or, as my deceased teacher, the philosopher Edmund Husserl, used to say by "Wesensschau" (intuition of essence). I believe that the exact reverse is true; objective statements about realities lying outside the region accessible to human beings without artificial aids, are only possible through physical observations and measurements. In the region of direct experience, which corresponds perhaps to the ontological "penetration to the essence", objective and subjective elements, psychological and physical experiences are interwoven and hard to separate. We must require of the concept space—time that it will not conflict in smaller regions with our subjective perceptions, our forms of intuition. This condition is fulfilled in relativity theory. We are not justified, however, in extrapolating directly experienced space and time into those dimensions which are so great or so small that they are only accessible to science and its instruments.

We have to make sure that any system of scientific concepts does not contain inner contradictions. It could be (and has been) argued against relativity theory that it is presumptious to maintain not only that the speed of light is the same for observers in relative motion, but that there simply is no other, faster vehicle for the transmission of signals (for the synchronisation of clocks): how are we to know that science will not, some time in the future, overcome this barrier? The answer to this is: the system of physics developed from this assumption is without internal contradictions. Its laws automatically ensure that no body and no group of waves with which one could signal, can be accelerated beyond the speed of light, because according to the very laws of relativity the inertial resistance (mass) increases with the speed and becomes infinite at the velocity of light. And this assertion has been confirmed by many exact experiences. We have, therefore, a logically and empirically well-founded system. If the future should produce something new, it will not be in a backward direction, as the foregoing objection suggests.

The above-mentioned assertion—that a returning space traveller would be younger than his twin who has remained at home—should not be called a paradox, but rather a scientific miracle in the same sense that one speaks of the miracle of radio and television, or, in another sphere, of the European economic miracle. There is nothing logically contradictory about it, but something definitely "wonder"-ful. According to normal biological conditions under which the human race has grown nothing of the kind would be possible. Twin brothers stay the same age; we can only speak to or see our fellow men if they are near us. To make it possible to see people a long way off as if they were near to us, miracles of thinking had to be performed. Let us be willing to acknowledge such miracles. Other types of miracle, e.g. the kind which contradicts the laws of nature, I shall discuss later.

From the standpoint of physics the dilatation of time is theoretically well founded and experimentally confirmed. It can be derived directly from the limitation of the velocity of signals, which could be demonstrated with the help of simple diagrams; but this would lead us too far astray. It has also been confirmed by exact experiments. For, although a human being up to now cannot travel fast enough, there do exist particles which emit light with a specific period, or which are radioactive, decaying with a definite mean time of life. Direct observation of these particles in fast motion meets a difficulty—a well-known phenomenon, the so-called Doppler effect: If a source of periodic disturbances (sound, light) moves towards the observer, the observed period is increased, if it moves away from him, the period seems to be decreased. To avoid this trivial effect it is necessary to observe the light in a direction exactly perpendicular to the movement of the source. The experiment has been successfully performed (by Ives a.o.) and the relativistic alteration in the duration of an oscillation has been established beyond a doubt. Another method observes the time it takes certain radioactive particles, the mesons, to disintegrate. These characteristic life-spans are known through terrestrial experiments for relatively small speeds. The same particles, however, are generated by the impact of cosmic rays on the higher layers of the atmosphere, and attain enormous speeds. Many of them reach the surface of the earth. The time needed for the journey through the atmosphere is a thousand times that of the life-span of slow particles; they should have disintegrated on the way. This puzzle is solved by taking account of the dilatation of time; for a human observer the life-span of these particles has been greatly extended, just as in the paradox of the twins.

These examples again show that the discovery of barriers leads to the widening and deepening of our understanding, and opens up new avenues of thought.

IV. General Theory of Relativity and Cosmology

It is well known that Einstein generalised the so-called special relativity theory in order to include gravitational movements. Here, too, we can speak of an application of the principle of impotence. We are concerned with a re-interpretation of the well-known fact that all bodies fall with the same acceleration provided that all disturbances have been removed (air resistance, etc.). Einstein formulated this as follows: "An observer in a closed box can in no way determine whether an acceleration of a body in the box is caused by an external gravitational field, or by an acceleration of the whole box in an opposite direction through space free of gravitation." In this formulation, which is called the principle of equivalence, direct experience has been expressed in such a way that it describes the inability to distinguish between inertia and gravitation. Einstein then postulates that this inability is a law of nature, and thus arrives at his general theory of relativity. This is one of the boldest and most impressive achievements of human thought. The orbits of the planets are considered as the shortest lines in a space-time-geometry which differs from the school geometry of Euclid. Space itself is considered as curved, the curvature depending on the masses of the celestial bodies. The Newtonian system of concepts is replaced by a completely different one. The only known deficiency of classical astronomy, a tiny but firmly established divergence between theory and observation in the trajectory of the planet Mercury can now be explained without further assumptions. Other optical consequences of Einstein's theory have also been confirmed although with less accuracy. The fertility of Einstein's ideas is most clearly apparent in their application to the structure and origin of the stellar systems. I am tempted to give an account of these, but must restrict myself to one of Einstein's cosmological ideas which has a direct bearing on our theme of the barriers in the physical universe. It concerns the age-old question as to whether there are limits, in space and time, to the universe, and where they lie.

I shall not discuss the ideas of antiquity by which the heavens were thought of as crystal spheres to which the stars were fastened like lanterns. Ever since Copernicus the question has been seriously discussed whether there is a finite or an infinite number of fixed stars? There were good arguments on both sides. It was argued, for example, that the stars could not be distributed uniformly throughout infinite space as the sky would then appear equally bright everywhere. But the assumption that there is only a finite number of stars, and that they fill only part of space, also seemed impossible, and for this contradictory reasons were given: some people said that the pull of gravitation would make all the stars collapse into each other; others said that as the stars move they would behave like a gas which expands and flies apart unless confined in some container.

The Viennese physicist and philosopher Mach contributed an important idea to this discussion. The inertial forces which occur during aberrations from straight or uniform movements (e.g. the centrifugal force in circular movements) are, according to Newton, physical expressions of the existence of an absolute space. This did not satisfy Mach; he demanded that these forces should be interpreted as the effect of distant stellar masses as a whole. This principle of Mach stimulated Einstein to one of his boldest speculations, namely the idea of an un-limited but still finite world.

In order to understand the significance of this one must realise that, according to Einstein, space itself is curved. What does that mean? Let us imagine that we are not three- but two-dimensional beings who live in a two-dimensional world, on a surface. As we lack the conception of a third dimension we cannot visualise what is meant by "curvature" of our surface world; we can, however, determine that for larger areas our geometry diverges from that of Euclid. By measuring triangles, etc., we could assure ourselves that we live on a sphere. (Actually, our existence on the surface of the earth has a certain similarity to that of these surface-beings except that, unlike them, we can visualise a third dimension.)

Now Einstein thinks that our three-dimensional world is, so to speak, a sphere of this kind, a four-dimensional sphere, curved in a higher space inaccessible to us, and closed.

Then the world would have a finite extension, there would be a finite number of stars fairly uniformly distributed; the world would not have an "end", boarded up, so to speak, but it would still be finite.

47

This speculation was confronted by an amazing astronomical observation. The astronomer Hubble found that the entire system of fixed stars expands. This system consists of enormous agglomerations of stars, billions in each, one of which is our Milky Way or Galaxy, while others are so far away that they appear to us as small nebulae. The distance of these nebulae, which are also called galaxies, can be measured fairly accurately by spectroscopic methods. We can also determine fairly accurately the velocity of the galaxies in the direction of vision, with the help of the Doppler effect mentioned above, which causes a shift of all spectral lines towards the red or the blue according to whether the nebulus under observation is going or coming. Hubble found that all the galaxies are receding from us, the faster the farther away they are from us.

As it happens, Einstein's gravitational laws contain just such solutions as will correspond to this behaviour; they assert an expanding spherical world, corresponding in our two-dimensional analogy to a rubber balloon which is being blown up.

This consideration leads us directly to the question of a beginning: if we pursue the blowing-up process backwards, we arrive at an initial state of the world where all matter is compressed into the smallest possible space. We can calculate the approximate date from Hubble's measurements; and the radius of the spherical world and its mass from Einstein's theory. We find the age of the world to be approximately 6 billion (thousand million) years, the present radius $6\frac{1}{2}$ billion light years (the light year is a measure of distance, namely that which light travels in a year), and the density about 30 hydrogen atoms per cubic metre. For comparison: the age of the oldest terrestrial minerals is about one billion years, according to reliable radio-active measurements. Thus we have in this spherical world absolute limits to space and time, and a finite mass.

Most astronomers and physicists to-day accept this cosmology as well established. But it is by no means undisputed. There are rival theories, for example, the one by British astronomers (Hoyle and others) who regard the world as being in a stationary condition. Instead of a definite day of creation, continuous creation of matter throughout the expanding universe is assumed; this will be very small, well below any possibility of direct observation. A definite decision between these differing hypotheses will perhaps be possible in the near future.

Was there anything before the creation of the world? Has this question any meaning? Probably not. According to Einstein, space and time are concepts which cannot be separated from that of matter, and which have the familiar, relatively simple qualities only because matter is very thinly distributed; i.e. the distances between stars are extremely great. It is therefore possible that an extrapolation into a past of billions of years and an enormous concentration of matter is meaningless, that in such circumstances our current ideas about time and space would completely fail us. Here we meet a limitation to our physical picture of the world so far beyond our imagination that we had better leave it alone altogether.

V. *Predictability and Accuracy of Measurements*

Having discussed the boundaries of the macrocosm (space, time, velocity), we shall now turn our attention to the barriers in the microcosm, the world of atoms and elementary particles. We had best pause here for a moment, and ask ourselves how it is with our scientific and mental methods; if there are not barriers to be kept in mind here before we venture into the microcosm?

The mathematical methods of physics are based on the idea of the continuum. We assume the existence of points and moments without extension, of infinitely thin lines and planes. For the purpose of the arithmetic definition of a point on a line we give its coordinate, e.g. its distance x from a point o on the line, and we assume that this quantity x can be determined with infinite accuracy. If $x = 1$, or 2, or 3 units of length or if it can be expressed in fractions such as $\frac{1}{2}$, $\frac{2}{3}$, $\frac{7}{10}$, this seems harmless enough. But there are such things as the diagonal of a square, and if the edge is a unit of length then the diagonal is $\sqrt{2}$. Now the Greeks already knew that there is no way of expressing $\sqrt{2}$ as a common fraction. In order to be able to deal with such quantities the idea of infinite (non-periodic) fractions was invented. Logically two such fractions have to be taken as different if they differ in any one decimal. For example, two fractions may agree in the first 100 places but differ in the 101st; in that case they are mathematically different. This procedure makes possible a strict and relatively simple treatment of geometry and kinematics. Speeds, accelerations can be sharply defined; the laws of physics assume the form of differential equations, and these enable us to forecast future movements if the initial state is known. This kind of prophecy has proved itself particularly in astronomy.

Here we meet the idea of determinism, predetermination, in a precise mathematical form. If we could know the present position and speed of every particle of matter, and could calculate fast enough, we would then be able to predict the future for any length of time. It is clear that such powers of observation and calculation vastly exceed our human capacities, and that is why the astronomer Laplace (end of 18th century) spoke of a spirit or demon who can do all this, and whom the physicists try to imitate. Notwithstanding this unrealistic image of the future, the deterministic idea has held sway until present times, not only in physics but in the whole of natural sciences, and has greatly influenced philosophy. Here we have an example of one of those violations of limits to which the human spirit is prone and which usually lead to disaster. In this case the result was an exaggerated belief in the scientific method which was then transferred to other sciences with much less claim to it, such as history, sociology, economics, etc. These are not based on differential equations which permit of precise and long-ranging predictions; nevertheless, there were and are schools of thought, such as Marxist materialism, which claim to be able to predict, accurately and infallibly, the social and political development of humanity. What, in fact, is the truth about the possibility of prediction?

Laplace's demon can only fulfil his task if he can take absolutely accurate measurements. The laws of classical physics are of such a kind that the consequences of an event are determined for all time if all the data are given at the beginning with mathematical accuracy (as explained above). But we are human beings, not demons. We can only measure with finite accuracy, and that not even very great. The best measurements to-day give in general six, at the most seven decimal places. At first sight this does not seem to matter. The demon is, after all, a distant ideal, and if each generation increases the accuracy of measurements (as has happened in recent decades), one will approach it closer and closer. This may well have been the general attitude. But it is wrong. Actually, the matter stands as follows: Even the simplest mechanical process, a turning wheel, a swinging pendulum, starts with a small inaccuracy, and there is always a critical moment when this gets greater than the whole range of the movement. Such mechanical systems are called dynamically unstable. If the original inaccuracy is reduced the critical moment is delayed; but it exists all the same. An absolutely accurate measurement would be a demoniac, not a human, achievement. It is not only conceptually an abstraction which may well be called nonsensical, but it also contradicts the laws of physics, namely the kinetic theory of heat which I have mentioned already, and which it would be absurd to doubt. This theory shows that the average kinetic energy of a freely moving body, be it a single atom, a group of atoms, a molecule or a visible macroscopic body, depends only on the temperature and is proportional to it (except for very low temperatures). At a given temperature the movement is the greater the lighter the body (for the kinetic energy is half the mass times the square of the speed). Careful measurements need very fine indicators (levers, etc.). The thermal oscillations of these indicators set a limitation to our measurements, depending on the temperature. Exactly the same considerations apply to electrical measurements. Here, too, spontaneous oscillations of currents exist which depend on the temperature; one can hear them as noises in a telephone. It is clear that a current, to be measurable, must be strong enough to be distinguished from this background.

One can lower the limitation of measurability by working at very low temperatures. But absolute zero is inaccessible, so that the thermal limits to measuring can never be made to disappear altogether.

All this is classical physics. In the atomic domain other limits have been discovered of which I shall speak presently.

A French friend of mine, Léon Brillouin, says in one of his books that the poet Paul Valéry used to be enthusiastic about the poetic beauty, the cold and hard severity, and the magic of mathematics. How true, says Brillouin, what else are the forms of mathematics—points without extension, infinitely thin lines, etc.—but poetic figments? I would not go as far as that; for mathematics permits sharp and cogent reasoning, and has been, in conjunction with statistical ideas, useful and indispensable to physics. If I wanted to give determinism a literary name, I would call it "fiction". I am aware of the fact that some great scientists, such as Planck and Einstein, whom I admire, clung to the idea of determinism, and that even to-day, some distinguished scientists do so. I, too, took pleasure in this fiction until I realised that it is not a picture of reality.

VI. Atomic Science and Quantum Theory

The discovery of the atomic structure of matter involves another thought barrier, namely a limit to the idea of continued divisibility. A drop of water composed of 100 H_2O molecules still has essentially the same properties as water in a tumbler; but an individual H_2O molecule has not. It is a structure of a different kind; consisting, as the formula tells us, of one atom of oxygen, and two of hydrogen. Further investigation shows moreover that each atom has a structure: a nucleus and an electron cloud. The nucleus again consists of nucleons each of which is nearly two thousand times as heavy as an electron, and which are partly electrically charged (protons), partly uncharged (neutrons). Besides these stable elementary particles a number of unstable ones, called mesons and hyperons, have been discovered; these result from the collision of stable particles, and decay, after a short life span, into other stable and unstable particles.

Now we may well ask what gives us the right to call these particles "elementary", a word which means, after all, that they cannot be divided up any further. Here we meet another barrier in our physical thinking, and one which goes beyond atomic science as such. From the time of the Greek philosophers Leukippos and Democritos there has been a constant idea that by dividing matter one will at last come upon something indivisible, elementary; and modern atomic science has taken up this idea and realised it. It has been considered self-evident and axiomatic by many philosophers that the whole is larger than the parts. But this idea becomes problematical in the region of particles of high energy because of the equivalence of mass and energy as postulated by Einstein in his relativity theory. According to this, the mass of a body is, so to speak, concentrated energy; one arrives at the energy concentrated in a body by multiplying the mass by the square of the velocity of light. As this factor is enormously large a small change in the mass represents a very large change in energy. On this fact depends the production of energy by atomic fission which is technically exploited in reactors, and used in atomic bombs for military purposes.

Now according to Heisenberg, our reasoning should be as

follows: when two particles collide at great speed, the energy concentrated into a very small space at the moment of impact consists not only of the mass of the particles but also of their kinetic energy which can be greater, even much greater, than the energy corresponding to the masses. The particles resulting from the collision will have available much greater energies than those deriving from the masses of the first particles. Therefore particles can be produced which individually and collectively have a larger mass than the colliding particles, and this, actually, often does happen.

Thus the traditional axiom about division breaks down, as not the mass but the energy is conserved, and this manifests itself partly as mass, partly as kinetic energy.

It is therefore preferable to speak not of fission and fusion, but of transformations and conversions. The concept "particle" becomes questionable in this context; there is very little sense in wondering whether a certain particle is really elementary when it may well be found to be a compound later on. It will be best to call those particles "elementary" which appear and disappear at high levels of energy exchange. An exact definition will only be possible when we shall have a comprehensive theory for particles as concentrations of energy. Heisenberg has made a hopeful beginning here.

The exploration of atomic processes had already resulted at the beginning of the century in a failure of ordinary, or classical physics, and the need to replace it by something new, quantum theory. This is a system as clear and self-contained as classical physics, but differing from it in many features. For one thing, it does not allow any unequivocal interpretations with the help of familiar concepts; for example, a cathode ray behaves, under certain laboratory conditions, like a rain of particles with a certain number of particles per unit of time; under different conditions like a wave of a certain wave length.

This duality wave-particle appears everywhere, among all the elementary and compound particles. It is something entirely

54

new, and breaks through all the barriers of our usual thinking methods. It has been realised that this difficulty cannot be overcome within the framework of deterministic theories, and can only be reconciled with a mainly statistical theory. The question is not: Where is a particle? but: What is the probability of a particle being at a certain spot? In simple cases the intensity of the wave, measured in terms of the square of its amplitude, gives the probability of the presence of a particle.

Closely bound up with this is a new restriction on the possibility of exact measurement of certain pairs of data, which are called mechanically conjugated, such as coordinate and momentum (mass times speed). We may assume that individually each of these quantities is measurable with infinite accuracy. But their simultaneous measurement is restricted by the uncertainty relationship discovered by Heisenberg: the more accurately the one of the two data is measured, the more inaccurate the determination of the other one becomes; the product of the two inaccuracies never drops below a certain limit which apart from a numerical factor is the famous quantum constant discovered by Planck.

VII. Complementarity

Here again an apparently quite reasonable procedure is declared impossible, and this particular case of impotence has attracted much attention.

The reason for this can be found in the common assumption that each period of time must have a fixed duration, each length in space a fixed extension. Is this really so? If one is not too particular, it certainly is. This lecture lasts one hour, this man has lived for 82 years, such statements make sense. A note sounding for $\frac{1}{10}$ of a second also still has a meaning. If, however, I want to be more accurate and say, this organ note of 50 oscillations per second sounds for $\frac{1}{10}$ of a second, then, to be precise, this no longer has any meaning. For a pure note is a periodic oscillation, but if it has a beginning and an end it is no longer pure, but a mixture of pure periodic notes of a small frequency range—say between 45 and 55 oscillations per second. Quite generally, mathematical analysis gives the product of the impurity interval (here 10 per sec.), and the duration of the vibration (here $\frac{1}{10}$ sec.) as unity; if one diminishes, the other increases.

This fact plays an extensive part in the construction of apparatus for the recording or transmission of voices and music, such as the telephone, gramophone, recording tape, etc. A whole science, information theory, has grown up in order to deal with these technical problems.

The uncertainty principle of quantum theory is of exactly the same kind. Yet the connection between the uncertainty relations appearing in the transmission of signals with the help of periodic processes on the one side, and those established by Heisenberg in atomic processes on the other side is based on fundamental discoveries in physics: the discovery by Planck, that each amount of energy is associated with a certain oscillation number which is exactly proportional to it; and also to the similar discovery by de Broglie that to a motion of a particle with a certain momentum there belongs a train of waves with a wave number proportional to the momentum. The factor of proportionality is the same in both cases, the above-mentioned constant of Planck.

How to make these assumptions of quantum theory generally comprehensible, and how to put them into clear and unambiguous language has caused many headaches. The solution accepted by most physicists is due to Niels Bohr.

He says that the two quantities of a conjugated pair such as time and energy, position coordinate and momentum need, according to their definitions, quite different apparatus for measuring. For times and positions one needs clocks and rigid scales, for energies and momenta movable parts for registering. A detailed discussion shows that these two conditions exclude each other as a consequence of the very laws of nature we wish to study. Bohr calls two such concepts and the corresponding apparatus complementary. They never lead to contradictions but they complement each other.*

In consequence, physicists are forced to discard the assumption that it is possible to represent all aspects of a phenomenon by one kind of observation and one set of concepts. There are always at least two aspects of a phenomenon and we have to choose in each case which one to prefer.

Here the subjective feature of modern physics becomes particularly apparent, and this has led to objections from many of those who have been trained in the classical school.

I consider complementarity as an important idea which can shed light on quite a number of matters outside of physics. Bohr has discussed these problems thoroughly; I can only just indicate them here. They concern such pairs of concepts as matter and life, body and soul, necessity and freedom. Around these ideas the philosophical and theological battle has raged for centuries because men have always set their hearts on bringing everything into one system. Now the impossibility of this has become apparent even in physics, that most rigorous and simple of sciences; even here the complementary attitude to differing aspects is necessary. Hence we must expect this everywhere.

* In physical and philosophical literature the term "complementary" has been much abused; for this the somewhat vague formulations of Bohr are perhaps a little to blame. In particular the descriptions of a process either in terms of waves or in terms of particles have been called "complementary". This I consider quite misleading; for the concepts wave-particle do not stand in a relation of mutual exclusiveness and complementarity, but both are necessary for the complete description of a quantum mechanical situation. In the simplest case of single independent particles the intensity of the wave (square of its amplitude) represents the probability condition for the appearance of a particle. In more complicated cases where particles cannot be regarded as independent, and where transformations of one particle into another may occur, it is possible to describe the process "dually" either as waves or particles, but such types of waves cannot be visualised any more, and do not represent the probability of a state. This is determined by a quantity of a higher degree, whose square determines the probability of a state in terms either of corpuscles or of waves.

Most of the philosophical objections to the "Copenhagen" interpretations of quantum theory rest on a misunderstanding of these ideas which any physicist handles without difficulty.

57

In biology, for example, we investigate living matter by physical and chemical methods. For the description of life itself, however, a completely different language is used, in which concepts such as purpose, will, pain, joy, habit, etc., play a part. We may believe, of course, that these are physico-chemical reactions in the brain which we do not yet quite understand. Bohr, however, believes that if we try to understand them physically, by experimenting on the brain of the living organism, we disturb the psychic event under observation, and the goal is unattainable because the organism will be killed by the experiment itself.

Innumerable abstruse books and papers have been written about free will. Without it there is no personal responsibility, no right and wrong, no guilt and atonement. All our social thinking rests on the assumption that man can make free decisions. But how can this be reconciled with the laws of nature, the all-pervading causality? According to this, my action is, after all, simply the last link in a chain of causes and effects for which I cannot be made responsible. When determinism began to lose its hold it looked as if we might have found an escape from this conclusion. If chance governs the single event, then the will which is visualised as some sort of spiritual being, has the last word. But this is quite untenable; that spiritual being "will" would then have to be continuously on the watch lest he violate the laws of statistics. Bohr considers this a false postulate. There are two aspects of behaviour, the physical and the moral; they are complementary, and not reducible to each other.

I must be content with these indications, and shall only point out that physics itself can be looked at from a standpoint which is complementary to the usual one.

VIII. The Related Sciences

This standpoint amounts to regarding physics not as a collection of scientific methods and results but as part of the life of the human race. Here we find questions of a different kind about barriers and how to overcome barriers. I cannot possibly treat these fully here, but perhaps I can mention a few points. First of all there is the question of the demarcation of physics from other sciences.

As regards philosophy everything to the point is contained in the verse of Schiller which I have chosen as my text. The world picture of physics (in which I include, as I said before, all those sciences which deal with inorganic matter, such as chemistry, crystallography, astronomy, etc.) is the result of thinking about experience, about the hard object in space.

The ideas of philosophy, on the other hand, often exist lightly side by side, even if they appear as mighty, closely knit logical systems. Many of the ideas of physics have first been thought of by philosophers. We physicists are grateful to them; for we aim at a picture of the world which not only corresponds to experience but which will also satisfy the demands of a philosophical critique. However, our image of the world does not fit into any of the existing systems. It is neither idealist nor materialist, neither positivist nor realist, neither phenomenological nor pragmatical, nor in complete accord to any other kind of system. It takes from all the different systems what will satisfy most thoroughly its empirical findings. What gives us the right to exercise criticism and choice towards the profound thought-structures of the great philosophers?

We derive this right from the fact that experience in physics has taught us to be sceptical towards philosophical ideas, and that we have succeeded by our own efforts in forming new ideas and concepts where the traditional ones have broken down. As far as I know, no philosopher ever doubted that statements about simultaneous events are always significant, until Einstein showed this to be an error, and deduced a new theory about space and time from the behaviour of hard matter. I also never heard of a philosopher doubting the sense of giving

59

to each event a certain duration until quantum mechanics refuted this assumption (and other corresponding ones about extension in space, etc.), and arrived at new concepts; and there are many other similar cases.

It is just because I insist that physics not only has a practical task to fulfil (providing a basis for technology) but that it ought also to be thoroughly philosophical, that I refuse to be interfered with by philosophers, if they can do nothing more than quote the authority of great thinkers, be they Plato or Aristotle, Thomas or Kant, Hegel or Marx.

The layman imagines physics to be virtually inseparable from mathematics. We are certainly deeply in the latter's debt. All the same there is a very distinct barrier between them. For although many branches of mathematics have received their initial stimulus from physics, the activities of contemporary mathematicians are a game with abstract ideas and have nothing to do with real objects. They invent systems of axioms from logical or aesthetic viewpoints, and develop them into amazing structures. Sometimes physicists find in them something serviceable and use it. Sometimes the mathematical tool is so useful that we believe it to have provided the final answer to a physical problem. An example of this is the identification of physical space and physical time with the mathematical continuum. We have mentioned this before, and have shown how this identification went much too far because it contained assumptions not verifiable by experience. This case, in particular, is perhaps the best example of the difference between thoughts and things described in Schiller's verse.

We now come to the biological sciences. The points of interest here are those we have discussed above under the heading of complementarity. It would seem as if the methods of physics and chemistry meet with no barriers here, since the analysis of the structure of living matter gets broader and deeper, but all the same I do not believe that it will ever be possible to uncover the secret of life; for life is, after all, not just a natural process like the growth of crystals or the movements of planets, but reveals itself in the phenomena of feeling, willing, desiring, which in man rise to full consciousness, individually experienced. It is possible that the complex processes of genetics will be thoroughly explained; this goal is already nearly reached. We know that the chromosomes in the cell nuclei contain structures, the genes, whose spiral-like arrangements determine the inherited qualities, and these genes have been identified with a certain chemical molecule, called desoxyribonucleic acid. The completion of these researches promises to reduce the processes of organic development to the more readily accessible problem of how such spiral-like molceules can be formed. But will this ever lead to an understanding of consciousness, which appears at a certain stage of evolution, and which has risen in man to such heights that it made him set the concept of the soul beside that of the body? I believe with Niels Bohr that the concepts body and soul are complementary, and not reducible to each other.

I do not want to engage in a closer discussion of these problems on the fringes of psychology, as I do not feel qualified to do so. I only wish to say a few words about the so-called para-psychology, as this calls in question the very foundations of the natural sciences. It concerns, in particular, extra-sensory transmission of thought. Again and again men and whole schools come forward and claim to have proved the existence of such phenomena by controlled experiments. I cannot judge whether these experiments and their (mostly statistical) results are unobjectionable. But for several reasons I am sceptical. Firstly, the possibility of such a means of communication between certain types of people (mediumistic) would give them an advantage in the struggle for existence; but I have never heard of such people being particularly successful. Secondly, one would expect this ability to be to some degree hereditary, in which case it is hard to see why it did not spread widely in prehistoric times and so get stronger. Thirdly, it is incomprehensible to me that the sense organs should have developed and perfected themselves if they were not needed. I believe that here we have a scientifically disguised transgression into the dark land of mysticism.

Of these arts, which interpret human activity as an expression of consciousness, there is here nothing to be said, as they take little notice of the natural sciences; much too little; for the course of history in general, and nowadays in particular, is conditioned by the state of technology, and this again by science. A few words about this later. I must give some attention, however, to the delicate question of religion, on which I have touched already.

In my father's generation this question still was discussed with passion. Since then a sort of truce has existed in the countries of the West, while in the communist states of the East atheism has been made into the State religion. It is not advisable to blow on the embers of such controversies. But as I am talking about the limitations of our physical world picture I cannot but say that I do not believe in transgressions of the laws of nature. As these laws are of a statistical nature, and therefore allow deviations from the norm, I must define more clearly what I mean. The statistical deviations themselves obey certain laws. The miraculous events of religious tradition, however, are of a different kind, they lie on a different plane altogether; they are meant to prove something lying entirely beyond scientific consideration, such as the power of prayer, the intervention of divine power for or against certain men or nations. All this has been discussed so frequently and thoroughly that I need not go into it here. I only want to return once more to what I have said in another context; Nature is so miraculous and wonderful just because of its lawfulness, that a belief in the transgression of these laws seems to me like a profanation of the divine order.

But this is a wide field, and I would rather turn towards those limitations of science whose effects are linked with the life of mankind.

IX. *Social and Ethical Limits*

In my youth it was still possible to be a scientist without paying much attention to the practical applications of science in technology. To-day this is no longer possible; for natural science is inextricably entangled with social and political life. It needs large sums of money which it can only get from great industrial concerns, or from the state, and therefore the results of research can never be withheld from these organisations. In particular, nuclear physics, rocket research and space travel use up enormous sums. Nowadays every scientist is a member of the technical and industrial system in which he lives. Therefore he must also carry part of the responsibility for a rational use of his results.

This would be easy if scientific and technical progress were always beneficial. We are in the midst of an explosive state of development and cannot predict where it will lead us. It seems to me that technology generally—unfortunately I cannot say "always"—wants the good, but often creates the bad. A few examples: scientific medicine has made epidemics and illnesses harmless, operations painless, and raised the average life-span. The result is an enormous increase in the the number of human beings. Whether food production will keep pace with this is uncertain. If not, then from good has come evil—a " world without living-space".

Industry has raised the standard of living everywhere, diminished the burden and hours of labour, brought leisure and the possibilities of travel, cheap entertainment by radio, cinema and television. But it has also alienated man and nature, herded people together in large towns, substituted doubtful artifacts for healthy natural foods, and has polluted woods, rivers, and the air with dust, exhaust gases and refuse; it has exterminated beautiful animal species, and estranged man and art.

63

The bad consequences of technology can be overcome if everybody helps, including those of us who are scientists in the laboratory and at our desks.

Probably we would have stayed cool and uninterested towards these problems if one event had not shaken us out of our complacency: the atom bomb. For it threatens the existence of civilisation, even of the human race altogether.

Nuclear physics remained pure science without an inkling of the disastrous consequences in store, up to the time of the discovery of uranium fission by Hahn and Strassmann. But immediately afterwards nuclear physics became entangled in the tragedy of the Second World War, and it would be absurd to maintain that physicists played a merely minor role in it. No, patriots as they were, they took part, prepared the way for the technologists, and in the end advised the politicians and military leaders on the use of the superbomb.

I do not presume to pass judgment on my colleagues who acted in good faith and conscience. What I do want to stress is this: that it is becoming necessary to examine the ethical limits of our world view as carefully as the physical ones. Many of us are doing this already, although nobody relishes it very much; not from laziness, but because in moral matters there are no such exact methods and distinct criteria of right and wrong as there are in physics. For myself the decision was fairly simple as I have never worked in nuclear physics, much less taken part in the construction of the bomb, and I have spoken my mind often enough: that I consider the use of weapons of mass destruction (chemical, biological, atomic) to be criminal; that I do not believe in the theory of the deterrent, as the execution of the threat would mean suicide; that war as a means of settling political disputes has become useless because it would with great probability lead to the use of these weapons of mass murder, and therefore to the extinction of mankind; that the idea of the defence of the realm has become equally senseless; and that all this has to be dinned into people until they understand it and force their governments to act accordingly.

Finally I want to say that we scientists, whose work has brought about the present situation, feel we have the right as well as the duty to find the limits of the practical world view, just as we are used to delimit our theoretical viewpoint. In the main we agree, as many public declarations show—I call to mind the Declaration of the Eighteen of Göttingen, Linus Pauling's proclamation of the 9000, the Pugwash movement and others. But there are regrettable exceptions. We are searching for rules of behaviour, and we gladly accept instruction from those outside our circle who have grasped that this is a new, unprecedented situation. I would like to mention here a little book by Günther Anders, *The Man on the Bridge*, which in the form of a diary on a journey to Hiroshima gives a profound analysis of the problems of the atom age.

He calls the year in which the atom bomb fell on Hiroshima and Nagasaki the year Zero, the beginning of a new age which can no longer make do with the traditional ethical concepts, and must form new ones. The philosopher Karl Jaspers in his great book *The Atom Bomb and the Future of Mankind*, describes the situation in the darkest colours; he hopes for salvation by reason, an elevated way of thought, which he describes and appeals to, without making it clear what it is or how it can help. For, according to Jaspers, we can only choose between the totalitarian system of communism, and defence of our freedom with the help of atomic weapons which would mean destruction for all. He therefore demands a willingness to make this supreme sacrifice. In this he agrees with the representatives of other ideologies; I shall mention here * only the Jesuit Gundlach who represents the Catholic point of view, and who prefers suicide to subjection; and the journalist Schlamm who does not hesitate to advocate a preventive war in defence of Western civilisation, and who attacks the physicists

* These examples are chosen to suit the German situation.

violently because we are searching for other solutions. One of us, the British physicist and Nobel Prize winner P. M. S. Blackett, has given a short and striking answer to all this (in an article in the *New Statesman*, 5th Dec. 1959, p. 783): "Once a nation pledges its safety to an absolute weapon, it becomes emotionally essential to believe in an absolute enemy." He further says, "Not infrequently the thesis has been upheld that national suicide was preferable to defeat. It is essential to understand that, while individuals can commit suicide, nations cannot; what is meant by this phrase, if anything at all, is that rather than accept defeat, the few individuals composing a government of a country would be justified in acting in such a way as to kill everybody else". Blackett thinks that such talk is nothing but moral boasting.

This seems to me too optimistic a view. When well-known philosophers, theologists, and publicists express such ideas publicly, they influence large parts of the population who will then support the governments in their outdated policies.

I believe that we physicists have the right and the duty to think out these problems, which have arisen out of our research, in our own simple realistic manner, and then to try to inform public opinion. We have no comprehensive world-wide organisation for this task. But some of us are working towards this kind of social consciousness, and already our efforts are meeting with some success. The leaders of the great powers have realised the dangers, and are trying to act accordingly. The most successful generals of the last world war, Eisenhower and Montgomery, have declared publicly that in the face of modern weapons and means of destruction war has become meaningless. But there are contrary forces at work, and our efforts at a clear demarcation of the ethical limits of science must not rest. Then we may hope that the present crisis in the existence of mankind, caused by an unrestrained application of the fruits of physical research, may at last be overcome.

CHAPTER 4

PHYSICS AND POLITICS

I. Introduction

General Mueller invited me to talk to you about the links existing between the discoveries made by physics and the politico-military situation. After some hesitation I accepted. My reluctance resulted from the realisation that I am not typical of my colleagues either with respect to physics or to politics. The branch of physics—nuclear physics—with which we are concerned here, has never been the centre of my interest and I had nothing to do with the atomic bomb. Concerning politics—I was born in Germany, forced to emigrate, and became a British subject. Anyone who belongs to two nations and also to a world-wide science thinks and feels somewhat differently from a normal citizen.

If General Mueller is of the opinion that a physicist has something significant to say about the present world situation, he probably attributes this to the fact that physicists have several times saved their science from difficult, sometimes seemingly insoluble crises, by their ability to reverse their thinking, by making a complete about-face. The world of politics is now facing such a crisis, and although the questions concerned differ completely from those in physics, it should be worthwhile to examine the methods of thinking of this science. We physicists are, moreover, very willing to place our experience at the disposal of politics. For we are aware of the fact that the political crisis was brought about by our research and we feel greatly responsible. I shall come back to this point again.

II. Crises in Science

Modern science was born at the end of the Middle Ages when progressive thinkers broke with ancient tradition, began to observe nature and to question it by experimentation. In physics Aristotle's doctrine, which had replaced Plato's philosophy since the 13th century, had ruled supreme but had degenerated into scholasticism. Aristotle maintained that every terrestrial body rests in the position assigned to it by nature and, when removed from it, tends to return to it. Thus the free falling of bodies was explained by the assertion that their "natural position" is in the centre of the earth. Why a stone or a spear should continue flight, even though the force of the arm was expended, remained incomprehensible; they tried to explain it by the forward thrust of the air displaced but this was an unproved and scarcely credible hypothesis. For celestial bodies a uniform circular motion was accepted as the "natural" one. However, since some of the planets actually seem to move in more complicated orbits, a simple revolution was not sufficient, and they were forced to invent complicated epicycloids (i.e. wheels which move on other wheels). This was the artificial mechanism on which was founded the Ptolemaic system of astronomy, which assumed the earth to be in the centre of the universe. But even Copernicus could not do without the epicycloids in his heliocentrical system.

Around about 1600 the almost 2000-year-old theory of Aristotle was overthrown. Galileo did experiments to find out what motions there really are and he discovered the laws of freely falling and projected bodies. These observations showed him that the natural, force-free condition of a body is not rest, but uniform motion in a straight line. Forces cause deviation from it, accelerations.

At about the same time Kepler discovered by careful and painstaking analysis of the astronomical observations of Tycho Brahe that the orbit of the planet Mars is not a circle but an ellipse and that the motion in this orbit is not uniform, but follows a different law (Kepler's second law).

As a result, 2000-year-old, petrified ideas became obsolete. It was a complete about-face, which soon bore fruit. From Galileo's and Kepler's beginnings Newton developed his mechanics, which became the basis of exact science for the next 200 years.

But then new crises appeared, again in the terrestrial as well as in the astronomical domain.

To begin with the latter, physics became involved in apparently inextricable difficulties when the propagation of light on earth was studied using very accurate methods. Since light proceeds in a vacuum and penetrates the empty universe, it was believed that the latter was actually not empty, but was filled with a fine, imponderable substance, which was called ether. But then on earth, which revolves around the sun through the ether, an ether-wind must blow like the draught in a moving, open automobile. Although the drift of light thus produced is very minute it was possible to construct instruments, so-called interferometers, which were sensitive enough to detect it. But nothing was found. Experiments devised to detect an influence of the earth's motion on electromagnetic phenomena also failed.

From these experiments sprang the theory of relativity, which again afforded a complete reversal of fundamental concepts. Einstein showed that a vicious circle was hidden in our reasoning. In defining the speed of light the supposition is implicitly made that it has a meaning to say that clocks at places far removed from one another keep the same time. However, to check this assumption we have to know the speed of light which, according to the ether-concept, depends on the unknown motion of the observer. Einstein resolved this difficulty by introducing relative times which do not coincide for observers in relative motion to another, but which can be reduced one to the other by a mathematical formula. These transformations involve also the lengths of solid substances. Absolute space and absolute time upon which Newton's mechanics was founded, were thus given up and replaced by more refined concepts. We may say that space and time have become relative.

No physicist doubts nowadays that the theory of relativity is correct. The conclusions drawn from it have not only been proven by astronomical observations but also through numerous experiments in laboratories. One of these consequences is the equivalence of mass (M) and energy (E), which is expressed in the frequently cited formula: $E = Mc^2$, in which c stands for the velocity of light. This law played a great role in nuclear reactions and the atomic bomb and can thus be regarded as a connecting link between physics and politics.

The second crisis in physics goes even deeper. It started in 1900 with a harmless looking formula which Max Planck developed to describe the properties of the radiation emitted by a hot body. This was the beginning of the Quantum Theory which at present governs all of physics, especially the physics of the atoms and the elementary particles (electrons, protons, neutrons, mesons, hyperons). It means again a moving away from Newton's mechanics but in a different direction, perhaps even more radical than Einstein's revolution concerning the concepts of space and time. The basic concept which now is being discarded is the causality as formulated in Newton's laws, or more accurately: determinism. According to Newton every later (as well as every earlier) configuration can be calculated from a given initial situation using the laws of motion. In place of this accurate predetermination a much weaker kind of prediction can now be made; the theory allows only the calculation of the probability with which a configuration is to be expected. That is, only statistical predictions can be made. The new laws of nature are such that they forbid the exact establishment of a configuration and, therefore, also the exact prediction of future observations. These new ways of treating natural phenomena, quantum mechanics and quantum field theories, have proved so satisfactory that there is hardly any physicist who does not use them or who doubts them. Differences of opinion exist only about the philosophical interpretation; but even here the great majority of physicists have accepted the ideas advanced by the great Danish physicist Niels Bohr. It is based on a consequence of Heisenberg's often quoted uncertainty principle, which maintains that certain pairs of quantities exist, for example the position coordinate, and the momentum (mass times velocity) of a particle which can never be measured exactly at the same time; if the accuracy of measurement of one is improved, the accuracy of measurement of the other would be lessened. Bohr illustrates this by discussing the behaviour of the instruments used for the measurements. For example, the exact determination of a position requires an apparatus with rigid parts, the measurement of an impulse requires a movable target from whose deflection the impulse of the particle under observation can be deduced.

To build an apparatus which does both is, as Bohr has shown, impossible. The instruments for measuring position and impulse are both necessary, they complement each other, they are complementary—a word which is also used in relation to the pair of quantities observed. This idea of complementarity appears to me particularly important, because it can be applied to other fields of thought. For instance, the eternal philosophical conflict over necessity and freedom of the will is thereby resolved; it is a question of two equivalent complementary aspects of the same situation.

I cannot go into greater detail. The purpose of this short exposition was to show that physics does not shy away from any revolutionary changes when the facts warrant it. The credibility of our methods of thinking is proved by successful results. This encourages us to enter the field of politics in so far as we are involved in it through the consequences of discoveries in the realm of physics.

III. Physics and Technology

The link between physics and politics is technology. Politics is based upon power, power on weapons and weapons on technology. In our history books this is barely or not at all emphasised. It is made to appear as if everything depends only on the wisdom of statesmen and the bravery of soldiers. But the sharper sword, the harder shield, the faster war chariot, the bigger and better ship always played a role, often a decisive one. Without them, for example, the victory of the small Greek cities over the enormous Persian empire would have been inconceivable. There are many other examples of the importance of technical superiority in decisive historical events, particularly after the discovery of gunpowder. Most noteworthy are the conquests of Peru and Mexico by a few hundred European adventurers. Their armour, firearms and cannons decided the issue.

The forging of weapons was a handicraft in Antiquity and in the Middle Ages. The collaboration of scholars in producing arms is reported as a curiosity, as shown for example by the story of the great mathematician and physicist Archimedes, who took part in the defence of Syracuse against the Romans by the invention of war machines and was killed during the storming of the city. In the Renaissance great minds appeared, like Leonardo da Vinci, who were at the same time artists, craftsmen, research workers, inventors, and designers of weapons. Starting with Newton a rapid development took place, in which science and technology collaborated closely in the way we know to-day.

Can we understand this sudden, explosive growth? Is there a historical law behind this? Many historians deny that such laws exist at all, others have advanced definite theories about it. I recall the German historian Spengler who, in his once famous book *The Decline of the Western World* tried to prove that all civilisations run the same cycle, i.e. rise, flowering, and decline. The English historian Toynbee similarly tries to show parallel developments through comparative analysis of many civilisations. Karl Marx's historical philosophy claims no periodical repetition of similar cycles, but a progressive spiral, which leads necessarily from the primitive existence of prehistoric man to communism by way of feudalism, capitalism and socialism.

I believe such speculations to be fantastic and dangerous. The only kind of natural law which a philosopher can expect in human society is the statistical one, which proceeds from the law of large numbers (of individuals). The case which interests us here is the question of how quickly something grows which reproduces itself always in the same proportion. A well-known example is compound interest. When interest is always added to capital, the increase is at first slow, then faster and faster and finally becomes enormous according to the law of geometrical progression or of the exponential function. But this behaviour can easily be obscured in the beginning stages, when it is affected by chance fluctuations; suppose, for example, in the case of compound interest, that in the same account irregular deposits and withdrawals were to be made. Progress in technology is similar. It has a tendency to grow, as each invention and improvement facilitates the next step. But as long as fluctuations predominate, caused by the accidents of politics, by war, and economic strife, this growth will not be apparent. Such was the case until about 1600. Then the rise began, which became rapid from about 1800 on, and is breathtaking to-day. It will continue so, if a catastrophe does not put an end to everything.

As I am almost 80 years old, I have myself experienced about half of this technical period. In my youth the difference in the way of life from that of, let us say, Cæsar's time, appeared prodigious; but the differences of to-day's existence from that of my youth is incomparably greater, so great, that an enumeration even of the most important things is impossible. I shall discuss just one.

Technology has become the decisive factor in waging war. This was so already in the First World War when victory in the endless battles was mainly a question of superior material. The Second World War was decidedly a struggle of machines and technological organisations, and it ended in Asia with the dropping of two atomic bombs, which had come straight out of the laboratories of the physicists. From then on we have a push-button war: nuclear means for mass destruction, delivered by rockets, which are guided by electronic brains—not to mention chemical and biological methods for annihilating whole populations. It is not my purpose to dwell on technical aspects. I will only say that both great powers, the United States of America and the Soviet Union, according to reliable estimates, have so many hydrogen bombs that each one could exterminate the population of the other not once, but 10 or 20 times and the rest of mankind in addition. For the radioactivity released in a great nuclear war is sufficient to destroy all life on earth.

This indirect, total push-button warfare no longer has anything in common with earlier warfare, either from a technological or from an ethical standpoint.

IV. The Plagues of Mankind

Mankind has always suffered from plagues and catastrophes: conflagration and inundation, illness and pain, starvation and war. Since the scientific-technical revolution we have gained the upper hand over some of these. Conflagrations and inundations have become rare in civilised countries and are combatted by rational methods. The Peoples' Republic of China regards it as one of her first duties to prevent the terrible floods of the big rivers.

The fight against illness and pain is being carried on with

ever-increasing success by medical science. In Europe and America the great killers like plague, cholera, smallpox, etc., have vanished, and many other illnesses have become harmless. In my youth a visit to the dentist, despite laughing gas, which was available even then, was a torture. Not long before that an operation without anaesthetics was sheer hell. No words of gratitude can express adequately our debt to medicine.

Starvation has also been conquered in civilised countries— at least as long as they keep the peace.

In the world as a whole there still remains much to be done. Only about one-third of the population has enough to eat. Two-thirds are undernourished, and when we count those suffering from poor diet, lack of proteins, vitamins, etc., then we reach the shocking figure of 85 per cent. Medicine and hygiene, too, are completely inadequate in by far the greater part of the populated world. To mention only one figure: the expectation of life at birth in India is under 30 years, while in Europe it is close to 70, in the U.S.A. above 70. Enormous tasks lie ahead of us. They are complicated by the fact that the increase of population is colossal. At the present time the world population is about 2·8 billions and it is expected around the year 2000, that is in 38 years, to reach 5 or even 6 billions. However, these enormous problems are recognised and are being studied. They could probably be solved, if the last and greatest plague were not present, war and the tremendous expenditure on armaments.

V. War and Ethics

War and soldiering are as old as human history. They have their ethical bases like every occupation. For we need an ethical justification for all our activities.

When I say a few words now about the ethics of the military profession, I am aware that those of you who are soldiers have very likely thought about it more thoroughly than I.

I merely want to point out a few basic principles which appear to me to be the essence of military ethics and to examine whether they are still pertinent to present-day warfare. In my youth, in any case, they were considered inviolate; through the Geneva Conventions some had become integral parts of international law:

1. War is to be waged for the defence of one's own people and for the protection of women and children;
2. Chivalry towards the enemy, particularly towards the conquered, has to be observed;
3. The defenceless, civilians, and cultural monuments are to be protected.

What is left of these principles to-day? Little even in the First World War, in the second practically nothing. Some chivalry among pilots may have remained. But fighting was no longer limited to armies; it was aimed in increasing proportion at the interior of the enemy country, particularly at cities.

It began with Warsaw, then came Rotterdam, Coventry, and countless other cities, particularly here in Germany. Bombs made no distinction between soldiers and civilians; men, women, and children, the old and sick were equally exposed.

Thus an ethical low point was reached, which seemed to make a further decline all but impossible. And yet this did happen at the end of the war through the dropping of two atomic bombs on Hiroshima and Nagasaki. The destruction of whole cities, which previously would have taken a few hours and somewhat endangered the pilots, was now concentrated to a few seconds and without danger to the aggressor.

These bombs resulted from the fission of uranium or plutonium. Since then hydrogen bombs have been invented, which use the fusion of hydrogen nuclei. The bombs dropped on Japan are toys compared to these so-called thermo-nuclear explosives. Already the first ones which were tested amounted to a thousand uranium bombs, and there is practically no limit to their size and strength.

To this we must now add the science of rockets, which removes the pilot's risk. But the essential consideration is that defence of one's country, protection of one's family have become just meaningless phrases. In a great atomic war the crews of the death-dealing machines (one can hardly call them soldiers any more) have a better chance to survive than the civilians of the warring (or even of neutral) countries.

I can hardly imagine that a soldier could welcome this development. The victorious generals of the last war rejected the new kind of warfare as a means of political decision. Shortly after the war, my university, Edinburgh, granted an honorary doctorate to the Commander in Chief of Allied Forces in Europe, General Eisenhower. I remember very well his speech of acceptance. He said that he intended to see to it that people of his profession would in the future no longer be needed. And I believe that as President he tried to carry out this intention as far as it was in his power to do so. General Montgomery, who was Eisenhower's next in command in the European theatre of operation, and General MacArthur, the victor in Japan, have likewise said that modern weapons have reduced war as such to the absurd. So much for military ethics.

Theologists and philosophers, ever since ancient times, have disputed and are still disputing the general problem, if and to what extent war is in accordance with the teachings of the Church and how it can be defended on moral grounds. With the exception of small groups, such as the Quakers, Christian theology up to now has not rejected war in general but only "unjust war". This is a distinction which is incomprehensible to my scientifically trained mind. For if two parties quarrel, each one firmly believes that his own cause is just. Consequently, there has to be an impartial referee. This role fell to the Pope as long as he was still the supreme authority in Christendom. But was he always unprejudiced? Not at all, for he was not only the spiritual leader but also a temporal ruler. During the Reformation part of Christendom separated from him and no longer recognised him as mediator. Apart from this internal difficulty of Christianity it happened that more and more non-Christian powers appeared on the political stage.

The concept of a just war leads to a maze of confusion and contradictions. I would not like to pursue such general problems any further; I only want to state what my own position is and to speak of the present situation which is dominated by the means of mass destruction, the ABC-weapons (atomic, biological, chemical).

This technological development has taken mankind by surprise; its moral progress has not kept up with it and is to-day at an all-time low level.

The Viennese author Günther Anders has described it thus: Wir können mehr herstellen, als wir uns vorstellen können (our production has outrun our imagination). The effects produced with the help of our contraptions (for example the killing of millions of people with one hydrogen bomb) are so great, that we are no longer in a position to grasp them. The links between intent, deed, and effect are broken.

These words describe the manner of a push-button war in excellent fashion. We can express the same thing more harshly; modern means of mass destruction no longer deserve the name of weapons. They exterminate men as if they were vermin. This is the outlook of to-day's armaments and strategic planning. I cannot think of anything more immoral and detestable.

Destruction by guided missiles is, however, not only morally repulsive but from a purely rational standpoint more than debatable. For almost all ABC-weapons, especially the thermo-nuclear ones, have the characteristic that they strike back at the one who uses them. They would undoubtedly lead to retaliation by the enemy with the same or even stronger means, and moreover cannot be restricted to the enemy alone. Radio-activity released through nuclear explosions will be carried along by wind and endanger all life on earth without distinction between friend and foe, belligerents and neutrals.

VI. *Peace Through Intimidation*

Of course, leading statesmen and the military know about this. According to them, nuclear armaments therefore only act as a mutual deterrent.

To-day we live in this state of "peace through intimidation". It is clearly completely unstable. Any incident, any rash action, can unleash the catastrophe. Hence it is clear that intimidation is only efficacious when the determination exists to carry out the threat. Since this would mean national suicide, this determination is not credible. There are, however, people who maintain that everything is at stake for us and we must be ready for self-sacrifice, even for aggression. In this extreme position representatives of opposing ideologies are united. I may mention as examples from West Germany the Jesuit Gundlach, who speaks for the Catholic Church, the philosopher Jaspers, who claims to worship the goddess "Reason", and the journalist Schlamm, to whom apparently the political institutions of the West are so sacred that he advocates preventive war, which would probably destroy them.

There is nothing I can do with such fanatics, and I would prefer to quote an English physicist, Professor Patrick Blackett. He was originally a naval officer, took an active part in the First World War and fought in the battle of Jutland. He turned to physics after the armistice and did some very successful research on cosmic rays, for which he received the Nobel Prize. In the Second World War he won great distinction in the defence of Great Britain through the development of a method for the most rational use of all available forces, called Operational Analysis. His interest in military affairs continued, and he published two books about Britain's defence with the titles *Military and Political Consequences of Atomic Energy* (1948) and *Atomic Weapons and East-West Relations* (1956). In these Blackett discussed the problems of nuclear weapons from a purely technological and political standpoint, without paying much attention to the human side. For this reason these books seem to me to be unsatisfactory. Later he published a rather long article in *The New Statesman** in which he presents the problem of Great Britain's defence briefly with great clarity and does not avoid ethical questions. From a military and political point of view he advocates that the West should not shy from costs and sacrifices, in order to have a conventional army comparable to that of the East. He takes a particularly firm stand against the proclaimed strategy of Western defence plans to answer with nuclear weapons any Soviet attack, even if it were launched with conventional weapons. He says: "Within a few decades, most political, military, religious and moral leaders of the West came to accept as justifiable a military doctrine, which previously they would have denounced as wicked, nauseatingly immoral and inconceivable as a policy for the West." He then says that if this policy were implemented we need no longer talk about the 6 million victims of Hitler's gas chambers; and that the civilised West would sink below the moral level of Genghis Khan. In order to quieten men's consciences about military plans, which obviously envisage the killing of many tens or even hundreds of millions of men, women, and children of the opposing side—and of one's own, a fact which, however, is generally obscured—the other side has to be thought of as essentially wicked and aggressive. Blackett put it in this way: "Once a nation pledges its safety to an *absolute weapon*,† it becomes emotionally essential to believe in an *absolute enemy*." † I think that each of us has within him something of this belief in the absolute enemy, and not only we who are average

* 5th December 1959.
† My italics. M. B.

80

citizens but also many of the statesmen and politicians on both sides. I carried on simultaneously an extended correspondence with leading personalities in the East and West, with the Russian philosopher Suvorov and with the Federal Minister of Defence Strauss, and both more or less insisted on the idea of the absolute enemy, seen in each case from opposite sides of the iron curtain. This is also the position of the previously-mentioned preachers of self-sacrifice, Gundlach, Jaspers and Schlamm. Blackett also considers the idea that national suicide is preferable to defeat: he calls it sheer folly. For if the phrase "national suicide" means anything at all, it means that the few people who compose the government of a country could be justified in acting in such a way as to kill everybody else. He believes that this is just "moral boasting" and asks how many of the individuals who mouth these words would in fact individually commit suicide in the event of defeat— history suggests only a very few.

VII. *A Glance at History*

We know that the heads of both great powers, U.S.A. and U.S.S.R., since they have been willing to meet each other, no longer believe in the policy of cold war and the strategy of intimidation and are striving instead for a policy which may be described by the words co-existence, co-survival, and peaceful competition. The government of Great Britain definitely shares this view. But everywhere there are people and groups who cling to the old illusions either out of honest conviction or for business interests. For armament has been and is a sure and profitable business for industry; disarmament, however, is difficult and risky. That is why again and again threatening words are heard from Moscow or Washington even when the atmosphere in general is inclined towards peace.

Goodwill and understanding are just not enough in a world which has never before been so full of problems. Every one of us in Germany knows those which are closest to us: Berlin and the separation of Germany. In Asia and Africa there are threatening unsolved problems, which are more important to the world powers. How can a mitigation of the cold war be attained as long as none of these problems is solved?

Formerly war was the ultimate arbitrator. War between nuclear powers has become, however, impossible. The introduction of world government and a world court is useless as long as there is no world authority which has the power to implement the decisions reached. We are still far from it.

And so many politicians, not knowing any better, continue their customary policies. They take the view that human nature is unchangeable: since there always has been war, there will always be war.

No one can deny that during all periods of world history great decisions have been made by war. Think of the Persian Wars through which the freedom of Greece was saved, or of the Punic Wars which resulted in the destruction of Carthage and made Rome a world empire; of the Germanic invasions which caused the downfall of this empire. Perhaps I am not very gifted in history; but at the risk of offending my colleagues of the historical faculty, I admit freely that most of the wars, which I had to study at school in history classes, seemed to me superfluous, foolish, and meaningless. What was the cause of the endless Peloponnesian War between Athens and Sparta? Jealousy and some quarrel or other, which nobody except a professor of history remembers. But what was the result? An incurable weakening of the Greek cities which left them open to invasion and conquest first by the Macedonians, then by the Romans. In all these cases the war aims were represented as eternal and fundamental; frightful sacrifices were demanded and made for them; but in the end it is found that these aims were insignificant and ridiculous. Here among you, Catholics and Protestants are certainly sitting peacefully together. Let us not forget, however, that less than 350 years ago some discrepancies in the dogma of these faiths caused a war in central Europe, which was the most brutal ever waged until the modern barbarism of the World Wars. And what are the friendships and enmities of peoples? During the First World War Germany opposed Japan; in the Second World War Japan was Germany's ally. From 1939 to 1941 Russia was Hitler's ally, from then on his relentless enemy, and the alliance which then was formed between Russia and the Western powers soon after 1945 showed signs of crumbling and turned into the great conflict from which we are now suffering. And for these changing, short-lived friendships and enmities millions and millions have perished and priceless cultural monuments have been destroyed. Of what avail is the sacrifice of the elite of a people and of its national wealth, when within only one generation friend and foe are interchanged?

You have doubtlessly been horrified listening to this rather disrespectful attitude toward history by a modern philosopher-scientist. What is coming now is an attempt to apply to politics the methods of reversed thinking successfully used in physics, and to point out seemingly irreconcilable contradictions as complementary and reconcilable situations. But you are now doubtless objecting: "You are a rationalist, but the world is not rational; it is driven by emotions, and these are short-lived. Show us a formula for improving the world. Until you can do this we cannot believe that things could change. It is safer to have deterrent weapons than anything else which you can propose."

VII. *Conclusion*

Those who argue in this way think of the armament race as a tug-of-war, in which both adversaries are almost equally strong. But in reality both sides attempt to strengthen themselves constantly by increasing their team. However, even if the balance is thus precariously preserved for a time, the tension on the rope increases—until it breaks and both sides fall on their backs. Nowadays, we just do not have standing armies with traditional weapons as in earlier centuries, but rather an armament race in technological capacity and at a speed accelerated by fear of the opponent. In this there is no security; some time or other the rope will break.

Moreover, the armament race is financially ruinous even for the mightiest economy. In addition to this, there are many who advocate massive civil defence programmes. Pascual Jordan, who as a physicist correctly estimates the magnitude of the problem, has no new thoughts on the subject, but advances some very old ones which by tremendous magnification he presents as "reversed thinking". He proposes the construction of underground cities. Human beings are supposed to live like moles. This is ridiculous and fantastic. But if we were merely to think of the construction of bunkers the protection of a sizeable part of the population would mean a tremendous increase in defence costs, presumably much more than double, without anything being accomplished, in my opinion. Perhaps part of the population could be saved from immediate destruction, but not from slow extermination through radio-activity, starvation, or contaminated food. There are still to-day 30,000 victims of radio-activity in Japan as the result of two small A-bombs.

If, however, my judgment of all this were wrong, I am certain about one thing, namely that the policy of intimidation by nuclear weapons is profoundly immoral and repulsive.

In this respect I am in agreement with many of my colleagues in all countries. And since we feel in part responsible for the development of this situation, we have founded societies everywhere which discuss these problems and seek solutions. Moreover, for the past few years there has been in existence a loosely-organised international group, politically completely neutral, the Pugwash Movement (which has nothing in common with the World Peace Movement, an organisation strongly inclined toward communism). Pugwash is the name of a little town in Canada, birth place of the American industrialist Cyrus S. Eaton. When some years ago the British philosopher Bertrand Russell, supported by Einstein and other scientists, proposed an international conference of research scientists for the discussion of the situation created by nuclear weapons, Mr. Eaton offered to finance the project and placed his estate in Pugwash, his birth place, at their disposal. There the first conference took place, and several others followed at different places. One of the more recent dealt with chemical and biological warfare. The transcript of the proceedings of that meeting would make the most callous person shake with horror.

The purpose of these meetings is to refute the insane idea of absolute enmity between economic systems and ideologies and to form a basis by which each national group can influence its government in the direction of moderation. We want our noble science to be used only to serve man's welfare and not to be misused for purposes of outdated power politics. We also want to establish a basis by means of which the conflict of ideologies can be brought on to an intellectual level. I have told you how physics has succeeded in solving apparently contradictory situations and has resolved them into complementary ones. In politics and economics two systems oppose each other, one of which proclaims the freedom of the individual as a basic principle, the other the absolute power of society organised by the state. Could these not also be two complementary aspects of the same human situation? My previously mentioned correspondence with the Russian philosopher Suvorov, in which I sharply attacked dialectical materialism, has shown me that one can discuss such questions with communist theoreticians.

Naturally economic and political differences will not be eliminated in this way. Some politicians have been proud to practice an art which in America is called "brinkmanship". It consists in pushing any dispute in current politics to the brink of the abyss, nuclear war. The former American Secretary of State Dulles was a master of this method. But Dulles is dead and so is his policy. In conclusion I shall quote a few sentences from a speech of his successor, the former Secretary of State Christian A. Herter, to show you this: a speech which he delivered in New York on 16th November 1959, not reported in the German newspapers available to me. Herter said:—

Mr. Khrushchev has said that we need to develop a common language despite the ideological conflict to which he staunchly adheres. Many will find this hard to believe after the years of baffling doubletalk. Yet I believe that on certain fundamentals we can find a common language because we have a common interest.

That interest lies simply in the basic will to survive, shared by free men and communists alike. I think the Soviet leadership is reaching a conclusion similar to our own—that, unless the course of events is changed and changed soon, both sides face unacceptable risks of general nuclear war which would approximate mutual suicide.

He then spoke of the substitution of peaceful economic competition for the armaments race and concluded thus:—

It was much simpler when we could think in black and white terms of sheer confrontation with 100 per cent. hostile communism. Even to-day, though the present arms race is dangerous beyond description, it still seems easier to continue on the familiar path than to try to break new ground.

Thus it will take courage of a high order and strong nerves over a long time to construct a new relationship between the antagonists' systems. But that must be done if civilisation is to survive. It is nothing less than this immense and long-term project on which we are now engaged.

There is a complete coincidence between the ideas of this modern statesman with those which I, a physicist, have proposed to you here. This agreement of ideas springing from two separate worlds gives us hope that the human race will survive the present crisis.